LA LLORONA

HER KITH & KIN

Statue of La Llorona on an island of Xochimilco, Mexico.
(2015. KatyaMSL - CC BY-SA 4.0.)

LA LLORONA

HER KITH & KIN

John LeMay

DEAD HORSE HISTORY

A SUBSIDIARY OF BICEP BOOKS, ROSWELL, NEW MEXICO

Printed in the United States of America

LeMay, John.
La Llorona: Her Kith & Kin
ISBN 978-1-953221-08-7
Southwest—Folklore/Hauntings/Supernatural

For all the mothers who warned their children
not to play too close to the water's edge…

Pecos River in winter, by Donna Blake Birchell.

A NOTE FROM THE AUTHOR

*"There are also some who state that the llorona is an infernal spirit wandering through the world, and entering the houses of those who are to be visited by great misfortunes, especially death in the family; and a few say that she is nothing more than an old witch (*una vieja bruja*)."*— Aurelio M. Espinosa, "New-Mexican Spanish Folklore."

As I was working on *The New Mexico Book of Witches*, I decided to throw in a chapter on the Ditch Witch herself, La Llorona. She wasn't really a witch in my opinion, but some people seemed to think she was. And besides that, it seemed like it might be fun to research. It was, and now I wrote an entire book on her.

In retrospect, my infatuation with La Llorona began much in the same way as it did with Billy the Kid. Initially, as with the famed outlaw, I had no interest in La Llorona at all because I took her for granted. She was everywhere in New Mexico growing up, and for a while, my opinion was more or less along the lines of, "What's the big deal?" To me, La Llorona was a run-of-the-mill ghost. However, in researching La Llorona for the first time in doing *The New Mexico Book of Witches*, I was intrigued with how far back her history actually dated. For instance, I had no idea her roots could be traced to the conquest of Mexico by the Spaniards. Then there were her many and varied forms. Sometimes she appeared as a white mist that turned into a spectral woman; at other times she appeared either as a skeleton in a dress or as a woman with the monstrous head of a donkey. Even her size sometimes varied, with her growing to the size of a giant or occasionally appearing like a small-statured fairy or duende.

To say that the Wailing Woman's history is fascinating would be an understatement at this point. I've enjoyed getting to know La Llorona from a distance, and hopefully this book can provide you with a safe vantage point to do the same.

John LeMay

TABLE OF CONTENTS

INTRODUCTION
GENESIS OF THE LEGEND

L a Llorona, aka the Ditch Witch, is unquestionably the Southwest's most famous ghost. Tales of her spectral wandering and wailing span from Texas to California. And that's just in the United States. Her hauntings also extend to South and Central America, with the latter being her most likely point of origin. Perhaps that is one of the many reasons that La Llorona is unique. Generally speaking, a ghost haunts only one region, place, or building, but La Llorona is everywhere.

The tale of a woman who drowned her children on purpose or who lost them in the river by accident is widespread. Chances are that if you lived in the American Southwest or Mexico within the last two centuries, La Llorona came from your town or village. "Each village seemed to have a different version of La Llorona," Cleofas Jaramillo stated in her semi-autobiographical book, *Shadows of the Past*. In Jaramillo's case, in Arroyo Hondo, New Mexico, La Llorona was described as a woman who appeared shrouded in a white mist before growing taller and taller until disappearing from sight, after which only her moans and wailing could be heard. Basically every settlement with Spanish heritage had its own version of La Llorona—many still do.

Classically speaking, La Llorona has always been a woman in white said to lure children to bodies of water where she will drown them, just as she did to her own children years ago. Usually, most children were lucky enough to escape her clutches and lived to tell of hearing her wailing cries and maybe catching a glimpse of her ghostly visage. Whether real or imagined, La Llorona was a useful tool in keeping children from getting too close to rivers and irrigation ditches lest she snatch them.

Advertisement for 1960's *La Llorona* feature film from Mexico.

If not scaring children away from waterways, she might be found frightening potential adulterers in dark alleyways. As it was, La Llorona also appeared as a seductress in the night, tempting men away from their families.[1] More than a few stories had La Llorona causing men to quit drinking and turn to sobriety, too. It could even be argued that as time marched on, she more often frequented the highways than the waterways.

In terms of description, La Llorona typically appeared dressed in all white, though in many other variations she was draped in all black instead. In at least one, she was even clothed in yellow— interesting because the ghosts of Spanish folklore are always associated with the colors of white, black, or yellow. Occasionally, she was even seen riding a white horse. Usually, La Llorona had the shape and form of a normal woman, but sometimes she was short, like a *duende*, or unusually tall. One sighting placed her at nine feet in height. In addition to La Llorona herself, a few encounters even included her lost children. One Texas-based sighting, with no location or witness given, described La Llorona as a faceless woman in white carrying a baby.[2] Whatever deviations existed between the descriptions, the constant was that she always wailed and cried.

Noted folklorist Aurelio M. Espinosa thought the legend of La Llorona was unique to Santa Fe when he wrote of her in 1910, and also described her as dressed in all black rather than white. Nor was she associated with water in his rendition:

4. THE WEEPING WOMAN
The myth of The Weeping Woman (La Llorona) is peculiar to Santa Fe. A strange woman dressed in black, dragging heavy chains and weeping bitterly, is often seen after midnight walking about the dark streets or standing at the windows and doors of private houses.

Vague ideas are expressed about her, but many state that she is a soul from purgatory, desiring to communicate with someone, or obliged to atone for her sins by dragging chains and weeping. That any soul from purgatory or heaven can come down to earth to communicate with relatives and friends, is a widespread belief in New Mexico; and it is not strange that any apparition, real or imaginary, is looked upon as a wandering soul. When The Weeping Woman is heard weeping at the door, no one leaves the house; and finally she departs, continuing her sad lamentations and dragging heavy chains.

There are also some who state that the llorona is an infernal spirit wandering through the world, and entering the houses of those who are to be visited by great misfortunes, especially death in the family; and a few say that she is nothing more than an old witch (*una vieja bruja*). *The Journal of American Folklore* Vol. 23, No. 90 (Oct. - Dec., 1910), pp. 395-418

But where exactly did La Llorona originate? Historically speaking, a very long time ago—possibly back to creation itself. But, in terms of La Llorona entering the public consciousness, one of the first people to properly write about her was Manuel Elogio Carpio Hernández (b.1791, d.1860). Carpio wore many hats in his lifetime. In Mexico, he served as a doctor and a politician, where he acted as the President of the Chamber of Deputies. More relevant to this work, Carpio was also a poet who wrote the poem "La Llorona" in 1849. Carpio's poem seems to be the earliest published piece to refer to the specter according to researcher Stephen Winick, who translated Carpio's poem, originally in Spanish, in this way,

Don Manuel Eulogio Carpio Hernández.

Pale with terror, I heard it told,
when I was a child, an innocent child,
that a bad man in my town once did to death his wife, Rosalía.
And since then in the shadowy night,
the trembling, frightened people hear the sad whimpering of a
suffering woman,
whimpering such as she made in her agony.
For a certain time she ceases in her lament,
but then she breaks out in prolonged weeping,
and alone she traverses the streets.
She fills everyone with mortal fear,
and close by the river in the thick darkness,
she goes weeping, wrapped in her cloak.[3]

Hernández obviously constructed his poem via oral histories and stories he no doubt picked up over the years. After that, La Llorona went from being a strictly oral tradition to appearing in print from time to time. Prior to appearing in newspapers, it's possible that each area's "wailing woman" may have gone by a different name, but after La Llorona began appearing in print, perhaps the name spread. As such, thereafter, any boogey-woman or female ghost glimpsed in the Southwest or Mexico was liable to be labeled as a "La Llorona."

Spanish folklore was rife with spirits and monsters, but unlike boogeymen such as the abuelo or monsters like the basilisk, La Llorona survived into the 20th century unlike many of her compatriots. Some of them, like the abuelo, clung to life into the 1950s until fading from memory. But not La Llorona. Through oral traditions, modern-day supernatural encounters, and feature films, her legend continued to expand rather than wither away.

As just one macabre example of La Llorona's legacy, in 1986, a woman was arrested in Houston, Texas, for drowning two of her seven children in the Buffalo Bayou. The woman, Juana Léija, was a victim of domestic violence along with her seven children and wanted to end their suffering. When questioned by the police, she was said to actually identify herself as La Llorona.[4] That same decade, La Llorona was used by the city of Albuquerque, New Mexico, in an official campaign aimed at children to keep them out of the arroyos. The main slogan was "Ditches are deadly, stay away," and La Llorona was featured on some of the signage accompanying this slogan.

Ray John de Aragón related an interesting new development in the lore in his *La Llorona* book. Aragón reported, "A cult has grown in Teotihuacan, Southern Mexico, and Honduras in a half reverence, half idealism of La Llorona."[5] Perhaps quasi-similar to the Santa Muerte movement, Aragón related how a ritual is performed wherein La Llorona's followers try to bring up her spirit by singing a ceremonial song in her honor. The singer is typically a young man who beseeches her to appear before him in the form of her past, beautiful self. The hope is that in seeing her captivating beauty that the revelers will all be "taken by her to live in what they think would be an eternal bliss."[6]

To this day, her cries reverberate from the riverbeds of New Mexico all the way to the concrete waterways of Los Angeles. As such, La Llorona is one of only a few specters to survive into the 21st century, making the transition from folktale to modern urban legend. This is her story, along with her kith and kin.

Section Notes

[1] It's worth noting that, in stories from Mexico, La Llorona was sometimes able to mimic the voices of different women, specifically the girlfriends or wives of her intended victims.
[2] Moran & Treat, *Weird Texas*, p.17.
[3] Winick, "La Llorona," Library of Congress Blogs.
https://blogs.loc.gov/folklife/2021/10/la-llorona-roots-branches-and-the-missing-link-from-spain/

[4] Bitto, *Mexican Monsters*, p.80.
[5] Aragón, *La Llorona*, p.2.
[6] Ibid.

PART I

PRECURSORS OF THE LEGEND

"Lilith" by Carl Poellath, 1886.

LILITH & THE LILIN

SHE DEMON OF SUMER

Like all legends, La Llorona had to originate somewhere, but where exactly? Although some think she's simply a Spanish version of the European "Woman in White," the premiere she-specter of the Southwest probably goes all the way back to ancient Sumer. That's because La Llorona's true progenerator is most likely Lilith. Originally known as Lilitu in Sumer, she is better known under the name of Lilith from Jewish folklore. In essence, Lilith was the original she-demon. She's been a succubus, a vampire and other supernatural creatures over the millennia.[1]

Lilith, for those unaware, was Adam's rebellious first wife from Jewish folklore and Biblical apocrypha. Whereas Eve was created from Adam's rib, in Jewish myth, Lilith was created in the same manner as Adam from the dust of the earth. As such, she saw herself as Adam's equal and would not submit, and so she was banished from Eden to the ends of the earth. Out of jealousy, she hunted the offspring of Adam and Eve, thus making her the first she-demon and one of the premiere specters to prey specifically upon children. In other instances, Lilith was said to be the mother of all demons after sleeping with the angel, Samael.[2] While mostly apocryphal, Lilith was actually mentioned canonically in the Book of Isaiah, where she was compared to the screech owl.[3]

"Lilith" by John Collier, 1892.

Lilith's ties to birds continued through her underlings, called the Lilin, whose demonic aspirations centered on the destruction of the family unit in some way or another. Usually this was done in the form of killing an infant in the night or by seducing a wayward husband away from his wife. The Lilin were often depicted as bird-footed night demons that subsisted on the blood of infants and their mothers. As such, there's an undeniable link between female vampires, specifically those that preyed upon children, and birds. The Greeks had a very similar female vampire called the Lamia, pictured above.[4] It had a penchant for preying exclusively on children at night, and like the Lilin, transformed into birds. Having the body of a crow most of the time, the Lamia was later incorporated into Roman mythology as a Strix, a blood-drinking nocturnal bird.

Like La Llorona, Lilith had some interesting connections with water. Some texts indicated she was created on the fifth day of the Biblical creation before Adam. Specifically, Lilith was supposed to have been part of the life within the waters. Later, when Lilith split with Adam, she uttered the ineffable name of God to acquire the power of flight and escape. It was over a river in Egypt that she was confronted by the angels who threatened to drown her. Otherwise, though, Lilith was not widely associated with bodies of water like La Llorona.

To boil it down, Lilith is to Jewish folklore what La Llorona is to the Southwest. In *Lilith's Cave: Jewish tales of the supernatural*, author Howard Schwartz pointed out that, like La Llorona,

Lilith served two roles. Primarily, she was the cause of infant deaths, but secondly, she was often used as a temptress, luring husbands or men in committed relationships to stray to their doom. However, Lilith never served in both of these capacities in the same folktale; it was either one or the other. Interestingly, the same could certainly be said for La Llorona, who served both as fatal temptress and child-killer, but rarely, if ever, in the same story.

"The Fall of Man" by Cornelis van Haarlem, 1592. Notice how it depicts the serpent in the Garden of Eden as a woman, specifically Lilith.

Adam clutches a child in the presence of the child-snatcher Lilith. (Fresco by Filippino Lippi, basilica of Santa Maria Novella, Florence.)

Ultimately, it could be argued that La Llorona is essentially a continuation of Lilith. However, for whatever reason, this iteration latched onto the public consciousness and survived into the 21st century better than all her kith and kin. At this point, it might even be accurate to say that La Llorona has eclipsed the story of Lilith in the public consciousness—in the Western Hemisphere, at least.

Chapter Notes

[1] One translation of Isaiah 34 specifically chose to call her a vampire.
[2] Often associated with the Devil, or Lucifer, in stricter terms, Samael is a different entity, often serving as a destroyer in the Old Testament and sometimes as the Angel of Death.
[3] Isaiah 34: "There shall the Lilith repose, and find for herself a place to rest. There the hoot owl shall nest and lay eggs, hatch them out and gather them in her shadow..."
[4] From Edward Topsell's *The History of Four-Footed Beasts*.

WOMAN CHIEF

"It is dangerous to talk about Woman chief. She is the same as the boss of all the witches."[1]

*T*he Navajo have a figure that might be something of a La Llorona equivalent, although she's very obscure and more tangential to the Lilith legend. The figure is called "Woman Chief" and is sometimes erroneously called the goddess of witchcraft, who resides in the Navajo underworld. In Navajo lore, Adam and Eve were essentially called First Man and First Woman, and the duo were the first to bring witchcraft to the current world. Woman Chief was the first person to suffer witchcraft at the hands of the couple, and as such, became "the first ghost," again bringing to mind Lilith, who became the first wandering spirit. Specifically, in an appendix entry in Clyde Kluckhohn's *Navaho Witchcraft*, it was written that "[Woman Chief] was the first person to die and became the first ghost." In the same tome a subject identified as Father Berard explained, "Because she was a 'chief' she is the chief of ghosts to whom mortals must return to in time."[2] An important element of Navajo witchcraft is often the theft of the targeted individual's personal property, which then becomes a talisman of sorts used against them. To reverse the curse inflicted upon them, the item must be retrieved. It is thought by some that stolen items used in sorcery went to Woman Chief in the underworld. In W. Matthews' 1888 article, "The prayer of a Navaho Shaman," the author wrote that "a lost element [became] in possession of the goddess of witchcraft in the lower world."[3] Woman Chief also figured into one of the stories of the Navajo twin war gods, Nagaynezgani (*Slayer of the Alien Gods*) and Thobajischeni (*Kinsman of the Waters*). To aid a neighbor suffering the effects of witchcraft, the twins met at the Carrizo Mountains, in the center of Dinétah, and from there went to the San Juan Mountains, where humanity was said to emerge from the underworld. The twins descended into the underworld in search of Woman Chief, who was in possession of the bewitched item. To do so, they had to pass through a number of mythical lands and challenges before finally arriving at her abode. With their magic wands, they managed to abscond with the item back to the surface, and all was well. Apart from passing mentions in stories such as the one just related, Woman Chief isn't terribly well-known in folklore.

Section Notes

---

[1] Kluckhohn, *Navaho Witchcraft*, p.136.

[2] Ibid, p.244.

[3] Matthews, "The prayer of a Navaho Shaman," *American Anthropologist* (vol. 1, no. 2 1888), p.164.

2

AZTEC GODS

LA LLORONA'S AZTEC ROOTS

Transitioning from Mesopotamia to Mexico, the gods of the Aztecs were another huge influence in the cultural creation of La Llorona. For instance, some scholars have linked La Llorona to Cihuacoatl, the Aztec goddess of motherhood. Interestingly, Cihuacoatl would stalk the Earth appearing as a woman in all white. With a crib strapped to her back, she would wander the marketplace until she found an unattended child to steal. Eventually she would disappear, leaving only the crib behind, and in it would be found a type of flint knife used in sacrifices in place of the baby.

Per Fray Bernardino de Sahagún's *The Florentine Codex*, a history of Mexico compiled in the 16th century, Cihuacoatl was described in this way:

> And they also say that she carries a crib with her, as someone would who carried her child in it, and she goes to the market, among the other women. And disappearing, she would leave behind the crib. When the other women discovered that the crib had been forgotten there, they would look to see what was inside: and there would be a flint, like iron, of the rough kind with which they killed those they sacrificed. By this, they understood that it was Cihuacoatl who had left it there.[1]

Depiction of Cihuacoatl.

In *Latin American Mythology*, Hartley Burr Alexander pointed out the differing versions of Cihuacoatl:

> Among the earth goddesses the most famous was Cihuacoatl ("Snake Woman"), whose voice, roaring through the night, betokened war. She was called Tonantzin ("Our Mother") and, Sahagun says, "these two circumstances give her a resemblance to our Mother Eve who was duped by a serpent." Other names for the same divinity were Ilamatecutl ("The Old Goddess"), sometimes represented as the Earth Toad.[2]

In the same way that Lilith had her devotees, the Lilin, the cihuateteo were the servants of Cihuacoatl.[3] Specifically, the cihuateteo were the spirits of mothers who had died in

26

childbirth. The cihuateteo also had macabre bird-like characteristics, as they were depicted with skeletal faces and eagle claws for their hands. Like the Lilin, they were believed to abduct or kill children, seduce men to adultery, and induce madness and seizures.

While Cihuacoatl was singled out as a candidate for the inspiration for La Llorona due to her association with motherhood, scholar Robert Barakat proposed Chalchiuhtliycue, the goddess of waterways and storms, as another possibility. In addition to being the goddess of rivers and other waterways, she, too, was associated with motherhood. Not to be trifled with, Chalchiuhtliycue was even the goddess who helped destroy the world via flood according to Aztec legend. In the *Florentine Codex*, it was said that Chalchiuhtliycue "killed men in water, she plunged them in water as it foamed, swelled, and formed whirlpools about them; she made the water swirl; she carried men to the depths." However, this didn't extend to all men, but mainly the ones who made a living fishing or otherwise associated with water. It was said that some ceremonies devoted to this deity involved infant sacrifice on the part of the mothers. The last of La Llorona's possible Aztec influences was the goddess Coatlicue, who was the mother of Huitzilopochtli, the Aztec god of war. Specifically, she was said to weep for her son while he was away at war.

Some think that either Cihuacoatl or Chalchiuhtliycue embodied themselves at one point to warn the Aztecs of the coming Spaniards. For those unfamiliar with the Spanish Conquest, preceding the arrival of the Spaniards were eight omens spanning everything from fire in the sky to strange creatures appearing. The sixth omen occurred around 1509 when a wailing, weeping woman wandered the streets for several nights, crying out, "My children, it is already too late," or, "My children, where can I take you?" All who heard the woman were filled with a deep sense of dread and foreboding. Specifically, Book VIII of the *Florentine Codex* recorded that, "In the days of this same Motecuçoma it happened that the demon Cihuacoatl walked about weeping at night in the streets of Mexico. Everyone heard it saying: 'My children, woe is me that I must soon leave you.'"

In *Legends of the City of Mexico*, Thomas A. Janvier quoted a passage from a sermon of Fray Sahagún that referenced Cihuacoatl, writing, "Your ancestors also erred in the adoration of a demon whom they represented as a woman, and to whom they gave the name Cihuacoatl. She appeared as a lady of the palace. She terrified, she frightened, and cried aloud at night."[4]

In the same tome, Janvier also quoted from Orozco y Berra's text regarding Cihuacoatl, specifically that she "appears dressed in white, bearing on her shoulder a little cradle, as though she were carrying a child; and she can be heard sobbing and shrieking. This apparition is considered a bad omen."[5]

Depiction of the Wailing Woman from Book VIII of the *Florentine Codex.*

To hit home his point that La Llorona descended from these gods, Janvier concluded the following:

> This legend is not, as all of the other legends are, of Spanish-Mexican origin: it is wholly Mexican—a direct survival from primitive times. …La Llorona is a stray from Aztec mythology; an ancient powerful goddess living on—her power for evil lessened, but still potent—into modern times.[6]

Janvier's opinion aside, when the Spanish Conquistadors arrived in Mexico, they undoubtedly brought with them European concepts of female specters. Over time, the legends of the Spanish and the Aztec gods likely comingled until they birthed the legend of La Llorona.

Chapter Notes

---

[1] She was mentioned again in Book VIII of the *Florentine Codex.*
Specifically this was in association with Don Martín de Alarcón, Governor
of Coahuila in 1705:

> In his time, it came to pass that the demon that in the form of a
> woman walked and appeared, by day and by night, and was called
> Cihuacoatl, ate a small boy, who was in his cradle in the town of
> Azcapotzalco.

[2] Alexander, *Latin American Mythology*, p.75.

[3] Due to the similarities, one could argue that these Aztec goddesses
might have stemmed from the Lilith legend in some way or another.

[4] Janvier, *Legends of the City of Mexico*, p.163.

[5] Ibid.

[6] Ibid.

THE WOMAN IN WHITE
& THE BANSHEE

LA LLORONA'S EUROPEAN ROOTS

Before Cihuacoatl wandered the streets of the Aztec capital in the 1500s, in Germany the tale of "The White Lady" was already being spread and was published as early as 1486 according to some sources. Though sightings of the White Lady dated back to the late 1400s, the poet Kaspar Bruschius put pen to paper to first record her in his *Chronologia Monasteriorum Germaniae Praecipuorum*, written in 1552 and published formally at Sulzbach in 1682.

In his rendition of the tale, the main figure was Kunigunde, the widow of Otto, the Count of Orlamiinde, who died in 1340. Kunigunde had birthed the count two children and was described as being a voluptuous woman who wished badly to be remarried. When news reached Kunigunde that Albrecht the Fair said he would like to marry her if she didn't have the two children, she drove a needle through their heads, killing them. After, she blamed their deaths on disease. However, a short time later, she learned that Albrecht had been misquoted. It wasn't her children that Albrecht didn't want to deal with, it was actually her elderly parents. Beset with guilt, she sought out the Pope in Rome, who, as penance, made her crawl on her knees all the way from Plassenburg to Berneck. There, she became a nun at a local convent, and after her death years later, Kunigunde began to appear before the descendants of Albrecht, the Hohenzollerns, as an omen of impending death or other bad news for the family.

Infanticide is obviously the Woman in White's main tie to La Llorona in addition to spurned affections. A few women in white have ties to water, though, like Canada's iteration of the legend in the vicinity of Montmorency Falls near Quebec City. There a young woman was betrothed to a soldier, and after he died in battle, the woman donned her white wedding gown and flung herself from the falls to her death in the waters below.

But, just like with La Llorona, the Woman in White has many variants. A variation of Kunigunde's story came from Cologne, where a ghostly woman was spotted at the site of an old convent. In this case, the beautiful young woman was the daughter of a tanner who was rather picky when it came to her suitors. Eventually, she became enamored with a knight who came into their home posing as a journeyman tanner. He wooed the young maiden, got her into bed, and impregnated her.

Later, he shirked his responsibilities as a father, refusing to marry her. One day, as the knight rode through the streets atop his steed jeering at her, the woman came outside with their baby. She threw it at the feet of his horse so that he trampled his own child. Then she took him by surprise, drawing out his sword from its sheath, and stabbed him. After the attack, the girl was arrested and sentenced to death, though she hung herself before she could be executed. Thereafter, her ghost began appearing at the spot of the murder of her suitor and her child. Any man who spoke with the ghost was said to die soon after. To atone for the woman's sins, a nunnery was built at the spot of her father's home, or so the legend said.

North America sports many Women in White, or White Ladies as they are also known. A woman in white haunts Durand-Eastman Park in Rochester, New York, and is also known as the Lady in the Lake there. The White Lady of Avenel hails from West Virginia, her origin story being that she waited for her husband to return from the Civil War until she died. Notably, many of North America's women in white had origins well past the Victoria era, with several of them being the ghosts of young women from the very early 20th century. In any case, if they had hailed from the Southwest, they would likely just be considered another La Llorona.

After the Woman in White comes the predominantly Irish legend of the Banshee, or the woman of the fairy mound. Like La Llorona, the banshee was notorious for its shrieking and wailing, and glimpsing one was thought to herald or precede the death of a family member. Wraith-like in appearance, the banshee usually had long hair and a dress that flailed in the wind as she screamed. Their eyes were even said to look swollen from weeping and screaming.

Oddly enough, one of the best-known places to see a banshee in North America was the Badlands of South Dakota. In *Myths and Legends of Our Own Lands*, Charles M. Skinner wrote of what he called the Banshee of the Badlands. Typically, she appeared as a translucent, blue woman. When not screaming, she might even look beautiful, but when she screamed, her eyes turned to black pits of nothingness.

According to Skinner, the banshee haunted Watch Dog Butte and was likely the ghost of an Anglo settler killed by one of the indigenous tribes of the region:

> It may have been the white victim of a red man's jealousy that haunts the region of the butte called "Watch Dog," or it may have been an Indian woman who was killed there, but there is a banshee in the desert whose cries have chilled the blood that would not have cooled at the sight of a bear or panther. By moonlight, when the scenery is most suggestive and unearthly, and the noises of wolves and owls inspire uneasy feelings, the ghost is seen on a hill a mile south of the Watch Dog, her hair blowing, her arms tossing in strange gestures. [1]

Banshee illustration from Ireland.

While La Llorona's true heritage is predominantly Aztec, it's likely that the Spaniards brought some of these European ghost tales with them to the Americas in the 1500s and thus influenced the legend of La Llorona.

Chapter Notes

[1] Skinner, *Myths and Legends of Our Own Land*, pp.184-185.

PART II

LA LLORONA

THE WELL OF
LA LLORONA
THE WAILING WOMAN IN SPAIN

It is difficult to decide where La Llorona really originated in the western hemisphere. Undeniably popular in the North American Southwest, her roots still go down to Mexico, and from there, possibly all the way across the ocean to Spain. As such, it's entirely possible that the conquistadors brought the legend of La Llorona to the New World. Or, if not the entire legend itself, they certainly brought the foundation with them to help birth the La Llorona myth as we know it today.

Valerio García recounted the theory in *Tales of Witchcraft and the Supernatural in the Pecos Valley* that La Llorona originated in Spain rather than Mexico. As opposed to being a mother who had murdered her children, she was a woman wrongfully accused of witchcraft who had burned at the stake in Spain. Because she was innocent, the myth went that her descendants, even those who came to the New World, would hear her wailing cries for years to come. As such, García reckoned that since he never heard her wailing cries himself, he wasn't a descendant of the woman.

Stephen Winick, one of the more devoted La Llorona researchers, found an even firmer tie between La Llorona and Spain. "I'm happy to say I may have uncovered something of a 'missing link,' which answers this question while it solves the mystery of whether there were 'La Llorona' tales in Spain," Winick wrote in his essay "La Llorona: Roots, Branches, and the Missing Link from Spain."

José Maria León y Domínguez c. 1897.

The story, "El Pozo de La Llorona," was published in Spain in 1866 by José Maria León y Domínguez, a Jesuit from Cadiz. Using a narrative device common at the time of inserting himself into the story as a first-person narrator, Domínguez was visiting the small Andalusian town of Rota. During his visit, he heard tales of the ghost La Llorona, who was used to frighten younger children into behaving. Domínguez began asking the locals about the ghost's origin until he got a solid rendition from an old man who gave the following account.

The story occurred sometime between 1350-1369, when King Pedro the Cruel ruled villages like Rota with an iron fist. In King Pedro's stead was an equally formidable young ruler, the castellan, who lived in a castle overlooking the village. So cruel was this young man that it was rumored that he tortured and killed wayward youths. This rumor mattered not to the most beautiful woman in the village, Elvira. She was haughty, and as the daughter of a widowed fisherman, she wished to elevate her social status. Elvira succeeded in beginning a courtship with the young castellan and soon after disappeared. Worried, her father went to the castle and begged to see his daughter. Elvira opened a window high above her father, and looking down on him figuratively and literally, she proclaimed she had traded living in his old shack for residing in the castle.

The father went away in shame, knowing he had lost his daughter to an evil man. As it turned out, the sadistic castellan was even too depraved for King Pedro, who had the castellan hanged shortly after his marriage to Elvira. Feeling ashamed for her husband's crimes, now exposed to the public, Elvira committed suicide by throwing herself down a well. Ever since then, she has risen every night at midnight from the well to wander the streets, wailing and moaning until finally she reaches the castle. Therefore, the place of her death was called the Well of La Llorona.

Assuming that the intriguing tale originated in the period that it was set, that being the 14th century, then it predated the Woman in White myth that came about the following century in Germany. If this was indeed a real tale told throughout Spain, then the conquistadors and other Spanish settlers could have taken it to the New World in the 16th century. If so, it's possible that elements of this oral folktale fused with a real-life event that occurred during the conquest to be discussed in the next chapter.

La Malinche as depicted in the 1916 book
The Mastering of Mexico by Kate Stephens.

LA MALINCHE

THE REAL LA LLORONA?

"In Mexico's creation myth, La Malinche has become Eve," wrote Dr. Amy Fuller in her article, "La Llorona and the Days of the Dead."[1] In addition to being Mexico's Eve, La Malinche is also the best historical candidate for what could be the real La Llorona. A figure dating back to the conquest of Mexico, her real name was Malinalli Tenepal, and she was from the Tehuantepec region. Throughout the conquest, she served as Hernán Cortés's interpreter and eventually became his mistress, bearing him either one son, Martín Cortés, or possibly two children depending on the source. These children were significant for possibly being the first *mestizos*. Or, in other words, the true progenitors of the Mexican people today, being of Spanish and Aztec descent.

La Malinche is whispered by many to be the original wailing woman of Mexico who would go on to become La Llorona. As stated before, La Malinche bore Cortés at least one child, but Cortés was not going to marry his Indian mistress, and when it came time to return to Spain, he left her behind. Some legends stated that Cortés desired to take his son with him, but not La Malinche herself. In her grief, further fueled by the anguish of being rejected by her lover, she killed the child and then herself. Afterward, she committed suicide, and when her spirit fled her body, it cried, "Aaaaayy!"

The meeting of Cortés and Moctezuma II, with Malinche acting as interpreter.

A variation of the story went that Cortés was lured away from Mexico by a beautiful rich maiden from Spain. The King and Queen of Spain feared that Cortés would begin his own independent kingdom in Mexico; thus, they wanted him to return home and used a beautiful woman to lure him back to Spain. Cortés obliged and, in this version, decided to take his two children with him while leaving La Malinche behind. Therefore, the betrayed woman decided to kill the children rather than let Cortés take them away from her. Some stories said La Malinche drowned the children, while others said she stabbed them with a sacrificial knife. Yet another utilized both by having her stab them with a ceremonial dagger through the hearts and then toss their bodies into nearby Lake Texcoco. According to some variations, La Malinche either killed herself soon after or lived another ten years. In that version, she spent much of the next decade sitting on the shores of the lake, crying out to her children. "Oh, hijos mios!"

"Ever since, her ghost has been wandering, and people everywhere hear her cry of pain. People call her La Llorona," wrote John Bierhorst in *The Hungry Woman: Myths and Legends of the Aztec*. In truth, how La Malinche died for certain is unknown, and where facts are absent, folklore will run rampant.

For instance, in trying to trace the roots of Arizona's iteration of La Llorona, folklorist Betty Leddy came across an account from Nogales that stated, "Another Nogales report indicates that the 'weeping one' is 'a wife of Cortez weeping over the grave of Cortés.'"[2] Leddy came across a few other references that would seem to allude to La Malinche without mentioning her directly. Leddy recalled,

> Besides the reference to Cortés, only two other stories seem to have historical significance: A native woman who worked and lived "in the house of Montezuma" killed her three children and herself. Only the soldier father and "those close to him heard her blood curdling cry. She appeared as a white shadow close to the house where she killed her children & herself." The other story is about a native seamstress and a count who precipitated tragedy by abandoning her and bringing a socially acceptable bride to the New World from Spain. The ghosts of the mother and her child appeared to those present at the duel in which the count was killed.[3]

Even outside of being the possible historical inspiration behind La Llorona, La Malinche's life is undeniably fascinating and tragic. She was born around 1500 in the Yucatan Peninsula, where neither the Mayans nor Aztecs had complete control. Her parents were of nobility and named her Malinalli Tenepal.[4] This second name would prove to be prophetic, as it roughly meant "one who speaks with liveliness."

It's unknown how or why, but at the age of eight or nine, she was sold into slavery. If her parents gave her willingly or if she was kidnapped remains unknown. By adulthood, she had become fluent in several different languages, most notably that of the Aztecs. In 1519, Hernán Cortés arrived at Pontonchan, where the city leaders gifted him twenty enslaved women as a peace offering, La Malinche among them. All of the female slaves were soon baptized by the Catholic priests accompanying Cortés, and each was renamed Marina, hence why La Malinche was also known as Doña Marina. However, the other "Marinas" were not given the more honorary title of Doña. That was reserved especially for La Malinche, but only after she had proved integral to the conquest.

At first, La Malinche was given to one of the noblemen serving under Cortés. However, once Cortés realized that La Malinche could speak both of the major languages of the Yucatan Peninsula, he took her for himself to act as translator. Initially she was paired with one of the priests who spoke one of the native tongues of Mexico until she herself absorbed the Spanish language and could thus act as Cortés's translator directly. During Cortés's negotiations with Emperor Montezuma, La Malinche was always present and proved so invaluable that she was often referred to as Cortés's right hand. The Aztecs were also impressed with her and bestowed upon her the name of Malitzen, which was a combination of her birth name with a Nahuatl honorary title.

More important than the talks with Montezuma were La Malinche's negotiations with other tribes who wished to see the Aztecs defeated. In large part thanks to La Malinche, Tenochtitlan fell under Spanish rule by 1521. Supposedly, Cortés even said that next to God, La Malinche was the most important factor in his success.

Although La Malinche was acting on behalf of tribes suppressed by the Aztecs, because she led all of Mexico to eventually being subjugated by the Spanish, she went down in the history books as a traitor to many. To this day, slang such as *Malinchista* serves as an insult and indicates a person who prefers foreign things.

As stated earlier, historically speaking, La Malinche is thought of as the mother of the Mexican people because in 1522, she bore Cortés a son, Martín. As Robert Bitto put it in an article on Mexico Unexplained, "Martín Cortés was the first publicly acknowledged person of mestizo, or mixed-race, heritage in Mexican history. This is the reason why Marina is sometimes referred to as 'The Mother of Mexico.'"[5]

La Malinche was still with Cortés in 1524 when she traveled to what is today Honduras to aid in suppressing a rebellion. There was one problem with Cortés's coupling to La Malinche: he already had a wife in Spain. To get rid of La Malinche as amicably as he could, he married her off to Juan Jaramillo, one of his captains. And, in marrying Jaramillo, La Malinche technically became Spanish nobility with the rights and privileges thereof. Contrary to the reports that La Malinche killed her son Martín and then herself, most historians concur that La Malinche lived on, bearing a daughter, Maria, for Jaramillo in 1526. From the best that researchers can tell, it seems that La Malinche tragically died three years later during a smallpox outbreak, making her only around 29 years old.

reclinandose inocentemente sobre el regazo de Hernan Cortes

The first true La Llorona sightings in Mexico City, according to Luis González Obregón, began about the year 1550, roughly 20 years after La Malinche's death. On moonlit nights, a woman in white would walk through the city streets wailing and crying before disappearing into Lake Texcoco. Supposedly, the first identity proposed for the ghost was that of La Malinche, now full of regret for her dalliance with Cortés.

All things considered, just as La Malinche gave birth to the Mexican people, she also helped birth the legend of La Llorona as well.

Lake Texcoco as depicted in *Harper's New Monthly Magazine*, December 1855.

Chapter Notes

[1] Fuller, "La Llorona and the Days of the Dead," Mexico Lore.
https://www.mexicolore.co.uk/aztecs/home/la-llorona-and-the-days-of-the-dead-in-mexico-1

[2] Leddy, "La Llorona in Southern Arizona," *Western Folklore*, Vol. 7, No. 3 (July 1948), p.276. You may have noticed the first account made the woman a servant of Montezuma. In later years, La Malinche would be connected to Montezuma in folklore, which stated that Malinche was Montezuma's daughter given in marriage to Cortes. In stranger accounts, Malinche was Montezuma's wife, whom he married in New Mexico to the north. (See this author's other title, *Pueblo Magic in the Land of Montezuma*, for more.)

[3] Ibid.

[4] The first name came from their goddess of the grass.

[5] Bitto, "The Mysterious Doña Marina, the Most Important Woman in Mexican History," Mexico Unexplained (June 13, 2016)
https://mexicounexplained.com/mysterious-dona-marina-important-woman-mexican-history/

Detail from "Carved tree in Arteaga, Coahuila, with La Llorona."
Photographed by Gabriel Perez Salazar.

LA LLORONA
IN MEXICO CITY

THE TRADITIONAL LA LLORONA

"**P**robably the legend of 'La Llorona'—'The Weeping Woman'—has permeated Mexican folklore more thoroughly than any similar theme," wrote Bacil F. Kirtley in his piece, "'La Llorona' and Related Themes" for *Western Folklore*. He continued his opening remarks, stating, "So pervasive is the legend and so diverse are its forms that the geographical distribution of its variants was one of the key problems investigated by scholars attempting to define provisionally the folklore areas of Mexico."

And he's right. There are a multitude of origins for La Llorona in Mexico, like La Malinche, discussed earlier. And while historically speaking, La Malinche might be the real inspiration for La Llorona, in terms of folklore, that honor goes to a woman who probably never existed. Most likely, she was herself a pastiche cobbled together from La Malinche, various Aztec goddesses, and the Woman in White from Europe, among many other sources.

The woman's name was Luisa Haro. It is her story that presented the most basic version of the Wailing Woman without too many nuances. The account was published in numerous papers in the late 1880s and was notably utilized in Thomas Janvier's *Legends of the City of Mexico*. Although Janvier's version was the most widespread, a folktale published in newspapers in 1888 told the story best.[1]

The story began in Mexico City in 1584. Luisa Haro was described as both the most beautiful girl in Mexico and also the most modest. Originally born in Spain, Luisa had been brought to Mexico by her father at the age of ten. Tragically, her father died when she was only fourteen, and without a mother, she was now an orphan. Rather than selling her body in the streets, Luisa swiftly learned a skill with which to eke out a meager living. Specifically, Luisa made artificial flowers, often for churches, and lived in a little house she inherited from her father. It was located along a lonely street "almost like an alley, in the shadow of the cloister walls of one of the guilds that chiefly employed her…"

Mexico City in 1690.

The article went on to describe Luisa's beauty and the admiration aimed at her by gentleman suitors:

> Luisa was the despair of all the gay, dissolute blades of the vice regal court of New Spain. Her neighbors in the lonely by-street were wont to point her out with a strange admixture of feelings, uncertain whether to respect and recommend her severe rectitude, or to disparage her, as one who is denied the natural passions and pleasant frailties of humanity.

At the age of twenty, a suitable suitor emerged in the form of Nuno, Marquis of Montes-Claros. As stated earlier, the beautiful and reclusive Luisa had been the subject of neighborhood speculation for years. So, when she vanished from her humble abode, her neighbors hoped that the beautiful girl had finally gone away to start a family. These suspicions were confirmed when one of the neighborhood men had business that took him to the suburbs of San Cosme. There, he saw Luisa standing on the balcony of Montes Claros's mansion, "blooming and with sumptuous accessories…"

However, all was not as wonderful as it seemed. After six years, and in spite of bearing him three children, Luisa and Nuno were still not married. And nor was the mansion his one true home, but one of several that he owned. Instead, Luisa lived there more like a prisoner than a beloved spouse. "In face and form she was more beautiful than on the day she fled with Montes-Claros, but still was she not beautiful enough to keep the fickle fancy of the Spaniard," the story related. One night, when it had been over a week since Luisa had seen the father of her children, she decided to go out looking for him. Leaving the children inside asleep, she "shrouded herself in a long, dark, clinging mantle, left the house, and took her way to the central streets of the city."

Luisa walked to the family mansion of Montes-Claros and was shocked to find a celebration in progress. "Nuno was there in the midst of his guests with his proud, affected mother, and beside them a young girl, tall and handsome, in bridal raiment," the story said. Luisa's heart sank. Even though she feared the answer, she asked a bystander, "Do you know, friend, who is the young lady beside the Senor Marques?"

"Who should it be," the man began with a laugh, "but his novia—the bride he wedded this morning at ten o'clock in the Chapel of the Sagrario."

Without uttering a word, Luisa walked back home. Upon returning, she sought out a cedar chest that Nuno kept. Within it was several valuables, but Luisa had only one in mind. It was a beautiful, bejeweled dagger. She took it from the chest and marched upstairs "lighted by the pallid, ghastly moonbeams… to the alcove where her little ones lay sleeping, and drew aside the curtains."

"Your father has forsaken us, my darling ones," she lamented to her children, "and your mother would fain preserve you from the miseries that await you. To God I recommend your innocent spirits."

The article described the pivotal moment thusly,

> Then, one by one, slowly, surely, fatally, she thrust the dagger into the bosom of each tender little body. Only when the blood welled darkly up, staining the white night raiment, did the wretched mother seem to realize her dreadful doing. She gazed a moment at the heart rending vision, and then ran forth into the streets, uttering those frightful wails that for 300 years have continued to echo in the streets of Mexico at varying hours and seasons—when the soul in penance can no longer endure its torture, so the devout say.

As Luisa ran through the streets, her wailing cries naturally drew the attention of the authorities, who saw her clutching the dagger, still dripping blood. Luisa willingly told the law what she had done and was imprisoned to await execution. By the time the fateful day came, she had withered away with grief to the extent that she was unable to walk up the steps of the scaffold for her hanging. "The execution proceeded, but the decree of the law was done on a corpse, for ere the halter touched her Luisa Haro was lifeless," said the article.

That same day, Nuno, Marquis of Montes-Claros, was found dead himself for reasons unknown and was buried shortly after his honeymoon. The article concluded that for centuries thereafter, the "flowers on the tomb of Montes-Claros withered, seared, and the earth upon it dank and noisome, as if it were drenched and soaked with blood."

Still from *La Llorona* (1930).

In retrospect, Luisa certainly brings to mind La Malinche, the jilted lover of Cortés. That she used a dagger rather than drowning the children was interesting as well, calling to mind the goddess Cihuacoatl, who left a dagger behind in the crib of the infants she had stolen away. The fact that the author chose to describe it as a "dagger, a curious jeweled weapon" seemed to imply some ancient origin or mystical attribute to it as well. On that note, the author of the rendition just recounted was Yda Hillis Addis, who herself constructed her story from an earlier version published in an 1880 verse collection entitled *Tradiciones y Leyendas Mexicanas* by Vicente Riva Palacio and Juan De Dios Peza.

Thomas A. Janvier popularized the story further and had a slightly different version of it, stating that the Wailing Woman "had drowned all her children in the canals of Mexico City." Actually, one translation acted as though she had many children and repeated the process over and over again. At some point, her conscience finally got the better of her, and she took to the streets "weeping and wailing, clad in white."

A variant collected from Dr. C. Knowlton of El Paso, Texas, related a version of La Llorona that kept to Lake Texcoco in Mexico City. Seen only during the summer months for some reason, La Llorona was said to appear near the shore in the water, wailing and crying, enticing men to come to rescue her. As they did so, she drifted farther and farther into the lake until her rescuer reached her. Then, she would throw her arms around his neck and laugh as she drowned him, similar to stories of the goddess Chalchiuhtliycue.[2]

CALAVERA CATRINA

However, more often than not, La Llorona stuck to the streets of Mexico City, where she would be seen walking calmly rather than running and shrieking. The woman would be wearing a white petticoat with a white rebozo covering her head. That's because, notably, this iteration of La Llorona was depicted as a skeleton in a white dress, more or less. Janvier related:

Meeting a watchman or a lonely traveler, she would cry out for her children, then disappear. He would lose consciousness or go mad. An officer who coaxed her to cast aside her rebozo was rewarded by the sight of a skeleton; he felt "an icy breath" and fell, unconscious. Later, having reported the incident, he died. To hear her is frightening; to see, to stop, to speak to her is very dangerous.[3]

Ultimately, that of Luisa Haro is probably the premiere La Llorona legend and one of the simpler ones. And, as the tale spread outside of Mexico City and made its way north across the border, it would spawn many, many deviations...

Chapter Notes

---

[1] This particular rendition came from the *Wichita Eagle* out of Kansas on May 12, 1888.

[2] The origin story in the tale unearthed by Dr. Knowlton focused on a young woman had an illegitimate baby. In this case, rather than the mother, the father got the infant and drowned it in a small lake. The bereaved mother then drowned herself in the same lake.

[3] Janvier, *Legends of the City of Mexico*, pp.134-138.

La Llorona According to Dobie

One of the more popular portraits of J. Frank Dobie in his later years.

A nother author to popularize the Mexican version of La Llorona was Texas folklorist J. Frank Dobie, who often traveled south of the border on hunting trips. On these trips, Dobie hunted not only game, but, more importantly, stories. He recorded the version of La Llorona he heard in his tome *Tongues of the Monte*. In it, he witnessed a group of children gathered at the feet of an elderly female storyteller.[1] La Llorona was brought up not by the woman as a warning, but at the behest of the children, who wanted to hear again of the wailing woman. Her rendition had La Llorona originating in the Red Mountains. She, too, dated La Llorona to the time of the Spaniards, before Mexico won its independence.

Before becoming a wailing ghost, La Llorona was a beautiful, rosy-cheeked blonde who had married a man and had a daughter with him. But the woman also had an affair, and her suitor killed her husband in a gun duel. This the woman did not mind, for she preferred the suitor to her husband. However, her lover despised her little girl. Fearing that he might leave her, the woman drowned her daughter. Soon after, the authorities found out what she had done and sentenced her to be burned alive. The old woman explained,

> On the day of the burning all the people came to the plaza to see. They were all saying, "Poor little one", and she was weeping but still beautiful. There was much delay and it was dark before the fire was lighted. Then they all saw something white and bright, exactly in the form of a beautiful lady, fly out of the fire and go towards the river where the baby was drowned.[2]

The old woman explained that the reason that La Llorona was seen all over Mexico was because she searched all of Central America for her dead daughter. That was why she was seen in Durango, Guadalajara, Mexico City, and so on. The old woman claimed that La Llorona would sometimes appear as a passing cloud, out of which her wailing voice would come. The woman, or possibly just Dobie through his narrator, also used Janvier's account of the night watchman encountering the skeletal La Llorona in the streets of Mexico City. The tale was mostly the same, but the woman added that the skeletal face shined "as bright as a coal of fire in darkness and every tooth brilliant like the point of a ray of lightning."[3] La Llorona's breath was colder than ice, and though the man was able to crawl home and tell of his terrifying encounter, he died not long after. The old woman's La Llorona was definitely a harbinger of death, even said to be able to sniff out a corpse buried deep in the ground as she searched for her baby. The old woman also claimed that "Where men are hanged La Llorona comes, and one near such a place can feel her breath as she passes. At any place where bandits bury a dead man to guard treasure she appears also."[4]

Whether Dobie added in the following flourishes, as he was wont to do, or if the old woman really claimed these things is anyone's guess. In any case, Dobie's account of La Llorona concluded with the children asking the old woman if she had heard La Llorona's cries herself. "Why not? If I had not heard it, how could I repeat it to you?" she said and then launched into her own impromptu imitation of the wailing woman that sent the children running back into the hacienda.

Section Notes

---

[1] The only identification Dobie bestowed upon this character was "the old cigarette woman," who was devoutly religious and who, the locals thought due to her extreme age, could sense the presence of death.

[2] Dobie, *Tongues of the Monte*, p.78.

[3] Ibid.

[4] Ibid.

NEW MEXICO'S WAILING WOMAN

LA LLORONA IN THE LAND OF ENCHANTMENT

Whether La Llorona is more popular in New Mexico or Mexico is a tough call, but it's undoubtedly a close one. However, out of the United States, it is for certain in New Mexico where La Llorona reigns supreme as the state ghost when compared to Texas, Arizona, and the other handful of territories that she haunts. Each New Mexico town, city, or village has their own unique version of the specter. Typically, they were river or drainage ditch-based, but occasionally La Llorona had nothing to do with water in certain locales. In Abiquiú, for instance, she was said to have been a mother who grew so weary of her crying baby that she tossed it from the church balcony to its death. Thereafter, she roamed Abiquiú, mourning and wailing into the night.[1]

To the south, the Hondo Valley sported a more traditional, water-based origin for La Llorona rooted in flooding. The Hondo Valley version of La Llorona was created when a pair of twins were swept away in some raging flood waters, never to be seen again and leaving behind a very bereaved mother. The woman died soon after and her ghost has roamed the Bonito River ever since looking for the twins. Another variation had the mother failing to evacuate her family soon enough from the oncoming flood, making it more of a cautionary tale. In this story, the river was full of drowning livestock shrieking in terror. As it swept the woman's children away, the mother was faced with the likelihood of drowning if she were to attempt to rescue them herself. Out of fear, she let her children drown and then grieved so hard that she died soon after, becoming La Llorona.[2]

Tales of La Llorona in the Las Cruces area are widespread along the Rio Grande. There, she was simply said to have been a mother overwhelmed by her two children that she drowned in the Rio Grande when it was a mile wide. The only interesting variation to this La Llorona was that a faint greenish glow hovered over the riverbank as she wailed for her lost children, who she was sentenced to search for until Judgement Day.[3]

Rio Grande River

The Rio Grande near Las Cruces, depicted in a vintage postcard.

However, like in Abiquiú, Las Cruces also included a totally land-based version of La Llorona with a more unique origin. In *The Gold Lettered Egg & Other New Mexico Tales* by Ted Raynor, the author recounted the legend of "Why the Wind Cries out on the Mesa." The tale was collected at East Picacho School north of Las Cruces. This version of La Llorona presented an interesting variation of the Spanish folktale of a teenager wishing to go to a late-night dance against the wishes of their parents or guardians. It also flipped the usual La Llorona role of the mother killing the child and had the child killing its guardian. In this case, a teenage girl desired to go to a dance against the wishes of her grandmother, who could not find a chaperone to accompany her. The night of the dance, after her grandmother had fallen asleep, the girl poured warm lead into her grandmother's ears so that she could not hear her sneak out of the house. Unbeknownst to the girl, the lead poisoned and killed her elderly guardian.

When she returned home from the dance, the wind was howling, and she couldn't find her grandmother anywhere inside. The girl ran back outside and, in the darkness, saw the outline of a woman bent over in agony. It was never the wind howling that she heard, it was the spirit of her murdered grandmother crying in agony. The girl then ran through the hills herself, screaming and crying over what she had done. "That is why the wind cries out on the mesa on nights when the moon shines brightly. It is the girl, wandering and crying out her sorrow," the cautionary tale concluded.[4]

Winter Wonderland, Santa Fe, N. M.

A La Llorona origin story collected in Santa Fe in 1945 claimed that La Llorona was a young woman who lost her lover and went up to the mountains to mourn him. A heavy snowfall occurred and she froze to death. Thereafter, the woman could always be heard crying when the snow fell.[5]

Moving onto the state capital, Santa Fe's La Llorona sightings are more often than not of the land-based variety, or that is to say that the better-known ones took place on land. A witch-like La Llorona was sighted in the streets of Santa Fe in 1949 by a boy who was on his way home from a screening of

Frankenstein Meets the Wolf Man. As opposed to a beautiful woman in white or a skeleton in a dress, he described this La Llorona as short, only three to four feet tall, and with a wrinkly face featuring a long nose covered in warts. Like all the others, she wailed in a fearsome manner, hence his belief it had been the Wailing Woman.

Whether it should be or not, the spot in Santa Fe most associated with La Llorona is that of the former Public Employees Retirement Association (PERA) building. That the building is said to be haunted is no surprise since it was constructed atop an old graveyard. Actually, a few of the lower levels extend into the ground itself, which might explain why some claim to see hands reaching out to get them.

Women in the old Saint Michael's cemetery, Santa Fe, New Mexico, c. 1930. (NMHM/DCA), #056598.

There are so many ghost sightings in the building it's difficult to say which ones truly qualify as La Llorona since any female ghost might be given that monicker. Actually, one could argue that all the different varieties of La Llorona have haunted the building for a time, such as a tall, thin woman who caused a janitor to quit out of fear. Then there were tales of a short-statured woman in all black who always wore a mantilla. She was said to be the grieving mother of a son who died of smallpox while attending St. Michael's College. Supposedly, he was hastily buried to suppress fears of a smallpox outbreak, and his mother didn't learn of his death until much later. She was also never told where he was buried. Longing to take his remains back home with her and not finding them, the mother died of a broken heart. That's why today she still searches the area for his grave. Not exactly a La Llorona story, but it's certainly tangent.

Bridge across the Rio Grande, Albuquerque, N. M.

Albuquerque, New Mexico's largest city, associates La Llorona especially with the Rio Grande and local drainage ditches. One iteration of the specter is named El Yorone, the spirit of a mother who lost her child when it drowned in a drainage ditch.[6]

Taos entailed a particularly interesting La Llorona variation in that she had apparently decapitated her child. As such, her ghost could be seen carrying a headless baby and a bloody ax. Her wail was so loud it was likened to a train whistle and would resonate throughout the entire body, not just the ears. The version of La Llorona from Los Lunas was also particularly vindictive. In her case, she hated her children so much that she cut them up and fed them to the pigs! Later, when she died, Heaven rejected her and sent her back to earth to search for her children's remains.

A group of boys in Santa Rosa claimed to have encountered La Llorona one night while playing in an old, abandoned school building. Upon spotting a white, shroud-like ghost, the boys identified it as "a llorona" (implying they considered it a type of ghost as opposed to *the* La Llorona herself). The boys decided to chase the ghost and throw rocks at it instead of running away. The specter began to cry and grow larger and larger, so the boys finally ran. Upon returning to the village of Santa Rosa, one of the boys claimed the ghost had touched him on the head. As evidence, he showed that a patch of his hair had turned white. Men supposedly went out to find the wailing woman and could hear her in the distance but never saw her.

A local chapel in Abiquiú, the Santa Rosa de Lima Chapel, sported a sign that said the place was "Under surveillance at all times by La Llorona."[7]

Tales of La Llorona are so prevalent in Mora that some call the Mora River "La Llorona's Highway." In Mora's case, La Llorona was a bit more sympathetic, as a widow with three children to raise on her own after the passing of her husband.

Unable to face the burden without him, she drowned her three children and then herself in a family suicide. Since then, her spirit has wandered both the Mora River and local acequias, taking wayward youths with her into the spirit realm.[8]

The Mora Valley of New Mexico.

Las Vegas has the most interesting milieu of La Llorona origins, two of which were connected to lynchings. The first linked La Llorona to Paula Angel, the first woman legally hanged in New Mexico on April 26, 1861. The nineteen-year-old Angel had entered into an affair with a married man and father of five, Miguel Martin. Supposedly, when Martin told Angel he was ending the affair, she stabbed him in the back, killing him in March of 1861. Not long after, Angel was hanged from a cottonwood.

A Las Vegas old-timer, Frank Maloof, alluded to a connection between Angel and La Llorona. He told the compilers of *The Weeping Woman*, "There was a story floating around when I was growing up here, supposedly about *La Llorona*, that she shot a fellow in the heart and the judge sentenced her to die by hanging."[9] According to the rest of the story, the woman was taken to an area near Montezuma Castle called El Barrio de Los Ortegas. They had "La Llorona" with a noose around her neck ready to hang, but no one wanted to pull the rope for fear that she either would become La Llorona

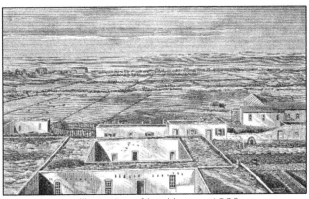

and haunt them, or that she already was La Llorona. In any case, the men let the woman go free. In a way, this tale suggested that any woman who was killed in a violent manner might later return as either the La Llorona or a La Llorona.

Better known was the sad tale of bandit Patricio Maes, who was hanged from the Gallinas River Bridge on a cold winter night until his frozen corpse was found the next morning. The hanging was an execution not by lawmen, but by fellow thieves in the New Mexico Society of Bandits, of which Maes was a member.

Image of unidentified woman often used over the years to depict Paula Angel.

Historian and folklorist Alice Bullock was one of the first to connect the killing to La Llorona, writing, "Over in Las Vegas the story is told that La Llorona is the mother of Patricio Maes, a bandido in Vicente Silva's gang."[10]

Illustration of Las Vegas c.1880.

Her 1974 newspaper article "La Llorona" stated that "Maes' mother is reported to have died soon after, and as La Llorona wanders up and down the Gallinas River crying out for her son seeking his murderers." An earlier source for the legend appeared in *Hispanic Legends from New Mexico* and had Maes's wife turn into La Llorona. The tale, collected in 1950, stated, "A man was caught by some gangsters and was hanged over a bridge. His wife would come to cry every day at the bridge. Now, after she has been dead for many years, people still hear loud crying at night by the bridge."[11]

Regardless of any connection to Maes, most of Las Vegas's La Llorona tales do revolve around the Gallinas Bridge. Another account spoke of "the witch that cries at the bridge between East and West Las Vegas has to come there at certain times because she killed her baby son and she is being punished."[12]

Illustration of the hanging taken from the *San Francisco Call* of July 3, 1898.

Another variant took place along Bridge Street leading to the Gallinas River Bridge every spring. "It is said that in the late 1800s, a woman's head was found in the middle of Bridge Street and no body was found to go with the head. The head was buried alone." The story continued, "Every spring, between twelve and one o'clock a woman's body without a head is seen and heard in Las Vegas. [The informant] has heard the cries of the woman. She has been named the llorona or 'cry woman.' It is said that she is looking for her head."[13] Another Las Vegas La Llorona tale had the wife of an abusive husband trying to run away with her two children. When she hid them beneath the Gallinas Bridge, they froze to death. Thus, she became La Llorona to wander the Gallinas in search of them.[14] Yet another Las Vegas La Llorona story had her as a skeletal woman in a veil picked up by a driver of the Lucero Taxi company. In that case, the skeletal woman jumped out of the cab while it traveled over the bridge.

Illustration from the
Albuquerque Journal
Of October 24, 1978.

Further north is Colfax, near the state line with Colorado, which hosts the ghost known as "the Weeping Lady of Colfax." Similar to the old woman who haunts the PERA building in Santa Fe, the Weeping Lady was said to be the mother of a son who died of an unknown illness in the late 1800s. Specifically, she haunted the back row of the old schoolhouse, which doubled as the church. In addition to her weeping, the cries of her son could also be heard along with phantom sounds of footsteps. Sometimes, she was also identified as a floating ball of light that traveled through town.

One of the most unique La Llorona tales from New Mexico came from the village of Anton Chico and associated her with fire rather than water. It was reprinted in *Hispanic Legends from New Mexico* and went thusly,

Once there was an old woman who had twin daughters. This woman loved her daughter so much that she would do anything for their happiness. One day she met an old wizard. The wizard asked her if she was in trouble. The woman said yes, that her daughters were starving and that she was trying to get food to save them.

The wizard said, "I will provide food for them if you will promise me that when they are 16 years of age you will give them to me."

The woman agreed, because she wanted to save her daughters from starving. The wizard provided food for them for four years. He came and took them away on their 16th birthday. The woman was very sad and wanted to look for her daughters but the wizard told her not to hunt for them, for he would burn her if she did. She didn't care about what the wizard had told her, so she started searching for them all over the hills and valleys. The wizard found the woman and told her that he was going to kill her. The wizard then built a big fire, tied the woman's hands and feet, and threw her into the flame, burning her alive. The blazes of the fire which burned her went up in a bundle and remained in midair.

They say that it was the spirit of the woman which held them together. The bundle of fire moved over the to the hills, still searching for the lost children. The people who saw it used to call it "la luz del llano."

Lover's Lane, a tree-lined grove that once existed in Roswell, was the haunt of a La Llorona-like woman in white.

Southern New Mexico has a few unique La Llorona-type specters worth mentioning as well. Otero County's La Luz has a more modern, La Llorona-like ghost that originated from a tragedy on a bridge.[15] One night several years ago, a mother and her two children were traveling across the bridge running over La Luz Canyon in their car when they were run off the road by a careless motorist. Their car crashed into the river, and the trio all died. Now, motorists crossing the bridge claim that they can sometimes hear children laughing in the breeze. They're ornery little ghosts, too, as it is said that if one parks their car on the bridge, ghostly forces will try to shove it off. A group of ghost hunters keenly aware of these tales decided to test this theory and put baby powder on their trunk. Later, they found small handprints as if made by children in the powder.[16]

Artist Neil Riebe's depiction of the Headless Horsewoman of Lover's Lane.

Although La Llorona was said to haunt the irrigation ditches of Roswell's East Grand Plains from time to time, a more famous female specter was the Headless Horsewoman of Lover's Lane. Lover's Lane was a shady tree-lined rural road northeast of town. It was said to have been haunted by a woman dressed in white riding atop a horse, only she had no head. The story went that she had been the daughter of a wealthy banker set to marry a local man, until he left her for another woman. One night, the woman, dressed in all white, came into her ex-fiancé's home and killed him and his new wife with a shotgun. After it was over, she turned the barrel on herself. The shotgun blast severed her head from her body, and from then on, her ghostly form terrorized young lovers along Lover's Lane until the old bridge she liked to haunt washed away.

The Concrete Flume of the Pecos River in Carlsbad, New Mexico.

Further south, towards Carlsbad, La Llorona would seem to haunt a stretch of highway near the ghost town of Seven Rivers. In *Haunted Hotels and Ghostly Getaways of New Mexico*, Donna Blake Birchell wrote that "Dale Balzano reports that the New Mexico State Police has told him that it considers the one-mile stretch of road in front of the tiny hamlet of Seven Rivers to be one of the most haunted stretches of highway in the state."[17] Although there were several specters said to dart into oncoming traffic, the most deadly one, and the one most frequently reported, was always a woman in white...

Chapter Notes

[1] In a strange flourish, occasionally she rode around Abiquiú on the back of a donkey that had its foot caught in a brass spittoon in an odd marriage of two local legends.

[2] Sanchez, "New Mexico's Weeping Woman," *Vision Magazine* (October 1, 1999).

[3] Hudnall, *Spirits of the Border*, p.141.

[4] Raynor, *The Gold Lettered Egg*, pp.36-37.

[5] Robe, *Hispanic Legends from New Mexico*, p.144.

[6] Hudnall, *Spirits of the Border*, p.61.

[7] Bullock, *The Squaw Tree*, pp.29-30.

[8] Interestingly, not only was she blamed for missing children in the region, but even missing livestock. One account had her dressed in sheepskin and entering a barn full of livestock. The next day, several animals were mysteriously missing from the barn.

[9] Kraul & Beatty, *The Weeping Woman*, p.23.

[10] Bullock, *The Squaw Tree*, p.30.

[11] Robe, *Hispanic Legends from New Mexico*, p.98.

[12] Ibid, p.96.

[13] Ibid, p.81.

[14] Kraul & Beatty, *The Weeping Woman*, p.18.

[15] Not to be confused with "la luz del llano" just mentioned, La Luz means "the light" and the place was named for an area ghost light that could never be explained.

[16] Hudnall, *Spirits of the Border*, pp.175-176.

[17] Birchell, *Haunted Hotels and Ghostly Getaways of New Mexico*, p.38.

LA LLORONA
IN ARIZONA

THE WAILING WOMAN
IN TUCSON & BEYOND

"The story of La Llorona has been told in Tucson for generations and the Wailing Woman served long as a local bogeyman," said Professor Frances Gillmor to the *Tucson Citizen* on December 6, 1972. In the early 1970s, Gillmor collected several accounts of La Llorona in Arizona. One account alleged in all seriousness that four female University of Arizona students had vacated a house they were renting due to it being haunted by La Llorona. As in most cases of poltergeist activity, doors slammed shut in the middle of the night and so on, but the blame was placed on La Llorona due to the fact that an unseen woman could often be heard crying and wailing outside. It was Gillmor's opinion that local pranksters were to blame, but because La Llorona was the de facto boogeyman of the area, one of the girls had likely heard the legend before and transposed it to the current situation.

Despite being a fairly arid region, most of Arizona's La Llorona cases still involve water in some way or another. One Tucson origin story for La Llorona was pretty standard in that it portrayed her as a mother who had lost her young son when he played too close to the river. Forever thereafter, the mother's spirit roamed the region, scratching at screen doors and leaving her fingerprints on windows in attempts to kidnap children to replace her dead son.

DEMONS, SPECTERS IN ARCHIVES
Professor Collects Haunting Stories of Wailing Ghosts

BY CHARLES HILLINGER
Times Staff Writer

TUCSON — Do you believe in ghosts?

Don't laugh. You might be surprised at the number of people who do.

Prof. Frances Gillmor, 69, one of the nation's foremost folklore authorities, has been collecting ghost stories for 30 years.

"These are stories related by people who swear they've seen ghosts, who gave vivid descriptions of the encounters and really believe in them," Miss Gillmor reports.

Hundreds of ghostly tales are catalogued and filed in the University of Arizona's folklore archives, maintained by the professor.

Southwest's Noted Ghost

La Llorona (la yor-ona)—"the wailing woman"—is by far the best known ghost in the Southwest. She's been around at least since the mid-16th century, a product of

Prof. Frances Gillmor
Times photo

The *Los Angeles Times* of October 31, 1972. The stories collected by Professor Gillmor helped popularize La Llorona in Arizona and elsewhere in the Southwest in the early 1970s.

Another of her many origin stories had her as a woman from Nogales, Sonora, who left her children behind in Mexico. However, when the Santa Cruz River flooded, the woman saw the dead bodies of her children follow her up the river to Tucson. Yet another Tucson old-timer attributed La Llorona to an old well near a deserted homestead where she cried every night at ten like clockwork. La Llorona's two main Arizona haunts seemed to comprise the Santa Cruz River and Tucson's Stone Avenue underpass whenever it would flood, though.

Little waterfalls along the Santa Cruz River in downtown Tucson in 1889.

Apparently, La Llorona was especially active during the flooding season. The *Record Searchlight* of November 7, 1972, wrote, "Whenever it rains in Arizona and the normally dry washes flood, people report catching a fleeting glimpse of La

Llorona or hearing her mournful cries." Clearly influenced by the La Llorona tales of Mexico City, it continued, "It's said that if you get close enough to her, you feel her icy breath. If her rebozo or her white gown is brushed aside, you see she is a skeleton — so they say."[1]

Per a folkloric survey in the late 1940s, Betty Leddy wrote in her essay, "La Llorona in Southern Arizona," published in *Western Folklore* (Vol. 7, No. 3) the following summary on page 273:

Out of thirty-nine accounts that describe either the original incident or the return [of La Llorona], fifteen connect the death with water, two mention her suicide in water, thirteen link her reappearance to water in some form. Sometimes the river is specified, e.g.: "Every time there is a big flood, in the Sonoita wash, it is said ..."; but sometimes the reference is vague, for example: "Now every time there is a big flood or that it is raining the llorona can be heard moaning and crying..." and "She... could be seen walking up and down along the banks of the river at night, crying". Even the well may be located definitely; for instance, on West Luna Street in Tucson. One story relates that a man on horseback, crossing a stream in Mexico, turned and saw "a llorona" seated behind him; he continued to the next town, where he told his story and died. A young Phoenician reports that "La Lloronanita" appears on the Phoenix-Tucson highway on stormy nights, carrying a cradle, stopping cars, asking "Where is my child?". A Tucson youngster told me that once he had wanted permission to watch stalled cars being towed out of a flooded underpass, but an elderly Mexican neighbor told his mother some woman would harm him if he went near the flood. He stayed away. La Llorona's reappearance near water is not difficult to understand if one considers the number of times the death she bewails was accomplished in water.

As in New Mexico, a notable number of La Llorona sightings in Arizona have absolutely nothing to do with water, though, such as encounters near the town of Patagonia. "Some people claim that they have seen a lady dressed in white and she has long, black hair. When they see her she is weeping. They have seen her out in the woods near Patagonia [AZ] and she has disappeared as suddenly as she appears," said one of the many stories collected by Betty Leddy in the 1940s.[2] One of the more elaborate accounts from the Patagonia area had a young ranching woman out in search of her cat. She could swear that she heard it howling in pain, but as she got closer, the cries turned into those of a woman's. She recalled the legend of La Llorona and so ran away to a nearby settlement where she collapsed and was unable to walk again for two whole weeks due to the shock and exertion. Others from the region locked La Llorona down to a schedule, claiming that she appeared only once or twice a year to sit on the banks of the river and weep.

The Santa Cruz River during the 1915 flood in Tucson, Arizona.

As with New Mexico's various wailing women, many of Arizona's La Lloronas were just female ghosts in general, though. A man from Tucson attributed a ghostly hand on his shoulder one night to La Llorona and high school kids blamed screams coming from the nearby hills on her. One account had teenagers in a car riding near an arroyo when a ghostly young woman appeared on their running board to hitch a ride. One of the more interesting stories came from a grocer who was walking along an unspecified river one night when he heard her tormented wails. The next morning, on the way to work, he claimed to find La Llorona's dead baby frozen solid, which he then exhibited as a tiny mummy in his store.

While many La Llorona tales naturally stemmed from the folklore of the distant past, a particularly interesting La Llorona incident sprang from Flagstaff's Santa Fe Dam in the 1970s. The *Williams News* of March 28, 1974, reported that the "Wailing Woman of Santa Fe dam" seemed "to be stirring lately." As it was, "a strange, wailing or moaning noise [could] be heard near the dam." The specter was never called La Llorona but was instead identified as "Lady Eudora," a ghost who wailed and cried over her dead baby who had drowned in the dam long ago.[3]

The Wailing Woman

(Continued from Page Five)

Gordon Wheeler responded to the call. The woman who phoned in pointed out to Wheeler where it appeared the sound was coming from. He searched around the house, a vacant dwelling, but found nothing unusual. He said that while he was still near the unoccupied house he definitely heard a moaning sound, as of someone in great pain. It seemed to come from up nearer the dam, and he immediately began a search in that direction.

In February, the police received a call "asking that an officer come to investigate a crying sound that was coming from a house near the dam." Police Chief Gordon Wheeler responded to the report and interviewed the caller, who identified the house from whence the wailing came. Wheeler himself admitted to hearing "a moaning sound, as of someone in great pain" in the area of the house. However, the noise seemed to come from nearer the dam, and so he set off in that direction.

It wasn't just Wheeler and the initial witness who heard the moaning, though. Two deputies joined in the hunt and heard the wailing, as did youths on motorcycles who rode through the hills trying to find the source of the noise. Nearby residents confessed they had listened to the cries before as well. Wheeler, for it was worth, was not aware of the tale of La Llorona and did not let it influence him. Furthermore, as opposed to simply hearing the wailing woman, a teenage girl claimed to have spotted a spectral woman dart across the road in front of her car near the dam once, and she had slammed on her brakes to avoid colliding with it.

Throughout the 1970s and 1980s, the *Tucson Citizen* ran stories on La Llorona, and invariably, their offices would be called a day or two later with a new La Llorona expert stepping forward. In his January 14, 1980 column, Don Schellie reported on one such call from a Tucson folklorist named David Huet. Actually, Huet had gotten his story secondhand from a University of Arizona-employed folklorist, Byrd H. Granger. It concerned what was certainly Arizona's most nuanced take on La Llorona. In Granger's unique variation of the tale, a drunken father was to blame for the death of the children rather than the mother.

Old postcard of Tucson, Arizona.

Long ago, in Tucson's southwest side, which comprised one of the area's poorer neighborhoods, a man stumbled home in a drunken stupor to find that his wife had gone out for the night, leaving the children alone. The man didn't know why his wife was gone for certain. For all he knew, she could have been out doing a good deed like tending to a sick neighbor. The drunk husband decided to assume the worst, though; that being that his wife was probably cheating on him. Worse yet, perhaps she would never return and had left him to raise the children alone. In a rage, the man killed his children, then took a butcher knife from the kitchen and hacked them into tiny pieces. So that no one would learn of his grisly act, he took the remains of his small children and buried them in various spots near the Santa Cruz River.

While the husband was still out, the mother returned to find her children gone and the house stained with blood. Knowing her children were likely dead, she fled the house, wailing and crying as she searched for them along the Santa Cruz River, her mother's instinct telling her that's where she would find them. She never did and died of grief within the week. What happened to the guilty husband has been lost to the sands of time. But the story wasn't over, not according to Huet, at least.

Modern image of La Llorona from Shutterstock.

According to Huet, for years, a series of unsolved grisly murders had plagued the Santa Cruz River, with various human remains in the form of severed limbs and headless bodies found in the vicinity. There were so many that the Tucson Police Department kept a secret file on the murders. "There is, [Huet] says, locked away at the Tucson Police Department, a very old and very secret file. No one, save the very top law enforcement officials, may read it, for it contains the case reports dealing with the many mysterious bodies that have been found over the years," the column reported. Of the unsolved murders, area residents knew that the real culprit was the ghost La Llorona. The article concluded:

But many of the old people of the barrios know the explanation.

It is La Llorona.

The old ones are convinced that the Wailing Woman still walks the banks of the Santa Cruz, and that she knows that her children cannot pass into heaven until their bodies are whole and...

Well, don't say we didn't warn you.

La Llorona chopping up bodies to replace her own children's missing limbs is certainly a unique addition to the legend and probably offered Arizona's best contribution to La Llorona lore.

Chapter Notes

[1] Other reports claimed that touching La Llorona might burn you instead of freeze you.

[2] Leddy, "La Llorona in Southern Arizona," *Western Folklore*, Vol. 7, No. 3 (Jul., 1948), p.273.

[3] If the drowning was accidental or on purpose was unknown, but that was the basic story.

LONE STAR
LA LLORONA

THE WAILING WOMAN IN TEXAS

Second to New Mexico, the Lone Star state probably boasts the most unique variations of La Llorona. Jack Kutz, who called La Llorona New Mexico's most famous ghost in *Mysteries & Miracles of New Mexico,* concurred in *Mysteries & Miracles of Texas* that "Texas' most renown spirit is, of course, the famous ghost-witch La Llorona."[1] Texas's version of La Llorona is quite different from New Mexico's, though. In one story, La Llorona was originally an Anglo settler rather than a Hispanic woman and, in many other cases, sported some kind of equine head, usually that of a donkey or a horse. Texas is also one of the only states in the U.S. to have a placename dedicated to La Llorona, that being Woman Hollering Creek off of Interstate 10, near Seguin.[2] It boasts the typical La Llorona tale of a woman who drowned her two children in the creek and who can now be seen and heard searching for them. Supposedly, her hand will reach out of the depths to grab onlookers who peer into the water.[3]

Woman Hollering Creek not only offers an Anglo slang placename for La Llorona, but a more Anglo version of the legend as well. In short, it claimed that a family of pioneers settled along the then-unnamed creek. When an Indian raid was due, the mother decided to drown her children in the creek rather than let the Indians either kill or abscond with them. When the Indians came upon the scene to find the wailing mother in the creek, her screams reportedly drove them away. Of course, there are variations to the tale, with one utilizing bandits rather than Indians as the marauders. Others still say that the story was made up after the spot was named. David P. Green, author of *Place Names of San Antonio: Plus Bexar and Surrounding Counties*, has said there is no definitive proof for Woman Hollering Creek's name. Furthermore, a more innocent explanation for the creek's name was simply that of a ranch wife whose voice traveled far when she would holler out that it was dinner time.

Although La Llorona sightings are spread throughout Texas, they are undeniably more prevalent in Bexar County and the communities surrounding San Antonio. A witness identified as Gene Sanchez, who served as commander of the Bexar County Jail, told how La Llorona scared him straight from a criminal past in *When Darkness Falls: Tales of San Antonio Ghosts and Hauntings*. In his early teens, Sanchez and two friends used to go prowling around at night and break into parked cars. Their stolen loot was stashed under a bridge along Camaron Creek. One day near dusk, the boys were under the bridge when they glimpsed a dark-haired woman in a white dress, combing her hair with an old-style Spanish comb. As she periodically dipped the comb into the river, she would wail and cry. Suddenly, she faded away, vanishing into thin air. Knowing they had seen a ghost, the boys all ran straight home. Sanchez told his mother about the incident and she asked him if he had been up to no good. Sanchez confessed to his crimes, and his mother told him La Llorona was a warning sent by God to put him and his friends back on the right path. She did, and the boys all grew up to be outstanding citizens.[4]

Castroville, east of San Antonio, hosted a typical La Llorona origin story in the form of a young woman courted by a rich suitor whom she did not wish to marry. As it stood, the young woman married the man only to please her family. Eventually, she gave birth to two boys, as was often the case with La Llorona. When both boys were still young, she began an affair with another man that she truly loved. When her husband found out, he left her to raise their two sons alone. Without his financial support, the woman struggled. Furthermore, her family was no longer around to help with her children either. Feeling overwhelmed, the woman snapped one day when she was picnicking with her children near the Medina River. She picked up the youngest, said to be three or four, and hurled him from a cliff into the river below. The older brother, horrified at what he was seeing, rushed to stop her. Unable to get there in time, he watched his little brother struggle to stay afloat in the water. His mother grabbed the boy as he ran at her and tossed him into the river as well. Neither of the boys knew how to swim, and both drowned.

Postcard of the Medina River.

In this version, the woman's lover didn't leave her after her murderous act—this La Llorona was smart enough to cover up her crime. Instead, she told him that she left her children with their grandparents. However, only a week after the children drowned, the man became bored with the woman and deserted her. Now with nothing left, the distraught mother had a mental breakdown. Unlike the undead La Lloronas, this one started her wailing campaign while she was still living. For two years, the woman, wearing all white, wandered up and down the river looking for the spot where she drowned her children. Those who saw her during this time claimed that when approached, she would cry, "I did it for him! They were my children!"[5]

During her two-year odyssey, the woman was said to have searched nearly every river in Texas until, finally, on the two-year anniversary of the murder, she found the spot along the Medina where her children drowned. According to some versions, she could see their ghosts playing happily along the shore. The woman then jumped from the same cliff she threw her children from to join them in death. A week later, the woman's body was found by her old lover, who had abandoned her years before.

If the woman rejoined her children in the afterlife or not is unclear, but her ghost was later seen in several different forms, one of which had the head of a horse—a means of punishing the once beautiful woman. Another was human, but she wore a black dress instead of a white one to show that she was in perpetual mourning. Another rendition put her in a red dress, meant to symbolize the blood of her children, which was odd since this version drowned her children rather than stabbing them as other variants did. La Llorona was also described as a ghostly, horse-headed woman in black carrying a lantern in Corpus Christi. This Llorona had an origin story quasi-similar to the one from the Medina River in that she tossed her children into a river, but in this case, it was because she was too poor to feed them.

In Lasara, a small town west of Raymondville, a witness in *Weird Texas* reported a land-based La Llorona sighting. In that case, a ghostly woman in white was encountered in an old abandoned ranch house. This version of the ghost was preceded by a windstorm and was seen hovering two feet over the ground. A gate at the ranch was said to open under its own power before she passed through it. The two witnesses drove off in their car only to have it die mysteriously near a bridge. Like a typical scene from a horror movie, as the witnesses tried to restart their car, the ghostly woman appeared again and floated towards them through a field. Eventually, the car started, and the witnesses got away to tell their tale.[6]

A wailing woman appeared frequently in the Fort Stockton area along Comanche Springs and in the St. Joseph's Catholic Cemetery, where she walked among the tombstones. An unnamed man had an encounter with La Llorona on a lonely highway near Fort Stockton one night in the 1960s. In that case, La Llorona appeared standing by the roadside then flew from the ground when the man sped past her. She then attached herself to the passenger side window and stared at the man for the next ten miles. No matter how much he accelerated or swerved, he couldn't shake the spirit who stayed glued to his car until she suddenly disappeared. The poor man would see the ghost nearly every time he took that road and, on some occasions, had passengers who backed up his claims. A year after the first sighting, the man was killed in a crash, leaving his friends to wonder if the ghost was trying to warn him or if it was the ghost who had caused the crash.

La Llorona possibly visited Henderson County in East Texas in 1915. The witnesses, Mr. and Mrs. Dearen, came along a bend in the road in their horse and buggy when they spied a curious woman sitting on a log. She was wearing a long, white dress and had dark-colored hair. The horse seemed to pay her no regard as though she wasn't there, and Mrs. Dearen wondered if only they could see her as they passed her. A bit later, they looked behind them. The log was still visible, but the woman was gone as though she never existed to begin with.

"I believe we have jest seen La Llorona," Mr. Dearen said, and his wife, knowing the lore, answered, "No, I don't think so because La Llorona is always weepin' and wailin'. I believe what we seen must of been some other kind of haint."[7]

Moving along to the borderlands of the Rio Grande, there is a woman in white who haunts Roma and has a detailed backstory. Like a few other La Llorona tales, it hinged heavily upon Catholicism. However, taking place in the mid-1930s during the Spanish Civil War, it was also a more modern affair than most La Llorona tales. It focused on a teenage girl named Isabel Salinas, who wished to join a local convent and did so as a postulant, or prospective nun. During this time, she met a handsome young man and fell in love. He was a Spaniard from San Antonio named Daniel Garza. Eventually, the two were engaged and Isabel received the convent's blessing to give up the sisterhood. However, Daniel had a desire to go overseas to fight in the Spanish Civil War in Spain. Though he claimed he would be back in time for their June wedding, Daniel eventually returned to Texas as a corpse in a casket. He had died fighting, and Isabela was inconsolable.

In a state of extreme denial, Isabela finished sewing her wedding dress and took to the streets of Roma every night searching for Daniel, who she believed to be alive—the corpse was a case of mistaken identity she hoped. Her family and friends could not stop her nightly wanderings, and eventually, she caught pneumonia and died. Thereafter, her ghost in the white wedding dress was seen wandering the streets of Roma looking for her lover to return from Spain.[8]

Postcard of San Benito, TX.

In the little town of San Benito, between Brownsville and Harlingen, is another unique La Llorona legend. It, too, was a more modern rendition taking place during the Mexican Revolution. Like many other La Llorona accounts, it had a well-to-do husband abandoning his wife and children, albeit with a twist. The burgeoning wailing woman was Dafne Bautista, the eldest daughter of a large family. Dafne's mother died giving birth to the family's sixth child, leaving the teenaged Dafne to take on the role of mother to her siblings. To help get by, she became a laundress like several other La Lloronas before her. She did her washing on the banks of the Resaca de los Fresnos, an oxbow lake.

There, she met her handsome suitor in the form of a Texas Ranger, Lawrence Woods, stationed in the area due to the encroaching tensions of the revolution. The two began a romance, and all in Dafne's family supported the notion of the couple being wed but one: Dafne's fifteen-year-old brother, Ovidio. To him, the Mexican guerillas of Pancho Villa were heroes and Texas Rangers were the enemy. Two years later, Dafne and Lawrence were married and had two infant sons. Dafne still worked as a laundress and often fretted over both Ovidio, who had fled to fight with Villa's men, and Lawrence, still in the Texas Rangers.

The inevitable tragedy struck when Ovidio and a group of revolutionaries were killed by Texas Rangers, Lawrence among them. It was too much for the couple to bear, and Lawrence left Dafne and his two sons behind to return to Houston, where his mother resided. Despite Lawrence's promises to send money to her and the boys, Dafne was understandably distraught at the tragedy that had befallen them all. Calmly, Dafne collected her two boys, telling them that she had to do some laundry at the lake. She loaded them onto a burro as she had done so many times before and set off for the lake. There, she told the boys they would take a swim before she did her work. Taking both of them into her arms, she waded into the depths until their heads were under the water and drowned them. Then, Dafne swam out into the deepest part of the lake and let herself drown.

The waterways of San Benito as depicted on a vintage postcard.

About to board the train, Lawrence had a premonition that something awful was about to happen. He rushed to the lake, knowing there his wife would be. Instead, he saw only the dead bodies of his boys floating in the water. Dafne was nowhere to be found. Lawrence took to heavy drinking and was eventually hit by a train as he wandered along some railroad tracks one night. That was only the beginning of the story, though. Sometime later, Dafne's younger sisters took over her laundry business and began to frequent the lake themselves. One night, the youngest sibling was walking along the shores when she saw her dead sister emerge from the water, wailing and crying, "Where are my children!?"

Dafne, either not recognizing her youngest sister, or perhaps not caring, seized her with her long fingernails and dragged her beneath the waves to her doom. The other girls would eventually follow, and thus began La Llorona's reign of terror at San Benito. Likewise, even Lawrence's ghost stalked the railroad tracks, making this one of the few instances where La Llorona's husband got in on the hauntings as well.

The El Paso iteration of La Llorona, being close to Juarez, was a bit more standard and derived from the legend of Luisa Haro, who had two children via a rich suitor in secret and later stabbed them when he married another woman. In the El Paso version, the unnamed La Llorona was a widow with two children from her previous marriage who lived in Juarez. When she entered into a relationship with a well-to-do man, she learned that the one thing standing in the way of another marriage was her children. Therefore, she took the two children to the Rio Grande River, which separates El Paso and Juarez, stabbed them, and threw their bodies into the river.[9]

The woman then went to the home of her suitor, with her white gown covered in the blood of her children. This she did intentionally, hoping to show the man what lengths she went to for him. The man was rightly horrified and turned her away. After this, the woman returned to the river where she either stabbed herself with the same dagger or drowned herself in the river, depending on the teller of the tale. Yet another variant also said that locals found out what she had done, and an angry mob carried her to the Rio Grande and tossed her in it.

This La Llorona was also one of the horse-headed varieties of the spirit. It was said that as punishment for her sin, she was given the head of a horse in the afterlife. Also distinctive to this version was that she wore the same blood-streaked gown. Like a demon or a witch, if one came across this La Llorona as she glided up and down the river, she might possess you. Under her spell, victims were unable to leave her and would end up drowning.

To this day still, anyone found dead or drowned in the Rio Grande is often thought to be a victim of La Llorona...

Chapter Notes

[1] Kutz, *Mysteries & Miracles of Texas*, p.32.

[2] An alternative name given for the location is Woman's Hollow Creek.

[3] Though based on real folklore, it was popularized in the short story collection *Woman Hollering Creek and Other Stories* by Sandra Cisneros, published in 1991.

[4] Williams, *When Darkness Falls*, p.299.

[5] Sceurman & Moran, *Weird Texas*, p.15.

[6] Ibid, p.17.

[7] Kutz, *Mysteries & Miracles of Texas*, p.33.

[8] This tale was likely a pastiche, cobbled together from local accounts, by David Bowles in *Ghosts of the Rio Grande Valley*.

[9] I assume she stabs them in this iteration so that her white dress becomes stained with blood to make for a horrific visual. Or, it could have simply derived from earlier legends where she also stabbed her children before tossing them into the river.

LADY OF THE RIVER OF SORROWS

LA LLORONA IN COLORADO

Colorado has many La Llorona legends, although, for the most part, they are usually no different than those found in neighboring New Mexico to the south. However, the legend of the River of Our Lady of Sorrows is a notable exception worthy of examination. The river was prophetically named by two Spanish priests, Francisco Anastio Dominguez and Silvestre Valdez de Escalante. The duo had left Santa Fe, New Mexico, to journey to California in August of 1776. As they crossed the wilderness of Colorado, they saw the river and named it Rio de Nuestra Senora de las Dolores, or the River of Our Lady of Sorrows. Considering its name, it's no wonder that it became a haunt of La Llorona.

La Llorona is probably a more recent addition to the river's lore, though. Prior to the wailing woman, the river's ghostly noises and apparitions were attributed to a tragic massacre from the 1800s. A Ute tribe was camped at the confluence of Beaver Creek and the Dolores River on June 18, 1885, when the encampment, comprised of only women, children, and the elderly, was ambushed by Anglo men. The Ute men were out hunting, and when they returned to camp, they found it burned to the ground and everyone dead. That's why, for many years, ghostly screams coming from the river were said to belong to the victims of the massacre.

Another early legend based around the Utes, printed in the *Elk Mountain Pilot* of April 1, 1920, attributed the ghosts to the long abandoned cliff-dwellings nearby:

> And to one who knows the Indian legend concerning the fate of the ancient peoples of this region, it is, indeed, a river of sorrow. The Utes tell of the great war with these peoples, and of how the Indians were victorious killing all the Cliff Dwellers and throwing their bodies into the Dolores. The spirits of these prehistoric peoples went into the bodies of the fish, and to this day no Indian will eat fish taken from the Dolores River.

Dolores River depicted on postcard.

Today, however, the ghostly wailing has been blamed on La Llorona, given her own unique origin story for the river. Sounding like the "howls of a tortured toad on a hot skillet"[1] according to author Stephanie Waters in *Colorado Legends & Lore*, La Llorona has been haunting the river for many years. Long ago, there was said to be a pretty senorita living in the village of Durango. She had begun a relationship with a suitor whom her parents did not approve of, necessitating that they elope. They did and moved to a small shack along the Dolores

River, where they lived in poverty. After having five children, the once beautiful senorita was showing her age and the husband decided to leave his family behind. Finding a new man to take care of her and the children was unlikely, and she was forced to work as a laundress who washed clothes along the river.

A lucky break seemed to emerge when she met a handsome Spaniard along the river. Not only did he sit atop a beautiful black stallion, but his fine saddle and clothes implied he came from money. The next day, hoping to better catch his eye, the woman adorned her hair with wildflowers and put on her best red dress. She was thrilled when she saw the man there again waiting for her. A steamy affair began, with the lovers meeting along the river each night. However, the woman never revealed to him that she had five little ones at home waiting for her. Not even after the man proposed to her did she divulge the secret. Knowing that her suitor would likely reject her upon learning of her five children, she made a very selfish decision.

The very day after he proposed, she woke her children in the middle of the night and marched them to the river. Due to being half-asleep, it was easy for her to drown each and every last one of them, letting their corpses drift down the Dolores River. So wicked was she that she didn't wail and moan like La Llorona, but instead laughed with glee. The next morning, her fiancé appeared waiting for her next to the river. All was well until suddenly from the water emerged five screaming children in the act of drowning. The man rushed to the river's edge, ready to dive in and rescue the children, who he still did not know belonged to his lover. The ghostly children vanished from sight before he could act to rescue them. Then, he watched in horror as his betrothed let out a bloodcurdling shriek and dived into the depths herself. She disappeared beneath the waves, never to be seen again. Not alive, at least.

The next night, a fisherman went fishing on the river as he always did. On the river's edge, he saw a crying woman standing there. When he reached out with a helping hand, the woman turned to face him. In her vacant eye sockets were squirming worms, mud clung to her black hair, and her head was bloated as though it had been submerged under water for some time. The woman let out a wicked laugh which sent the fisherman running to tell his tale. The story spread, and others began to see the apparition until it was finally bestowed with the name La Llorona.

After all those years, it could be argued that the priests' naming of the river had become literal, for it truly was a river of sorrows due to the actions of La Llorona.

Chapter Notes

---

[1] Waters, *Colorado Legends & Lore*, p.101.

THE WITCH OF
SNAKE ROAD

LA LLORONA OF CALIFORNIA

L a Llorona undoubtedly has a strong presence in the state of California. For the most part, California's La Llorona tales are no different than elsewhere other than that they are decidedly more modern and sometimes urban. For instance, 2019's *The Curse of La Llorona* had the specter haunting the Los Angeles Aqueduct system. While La Llorona haunting the concrete waterways could just be an example of the Wailing Woman changing with the times, what about a story where she and her children drowned in a car? Well, she did in California. Enter the Fresno County farming community of Sanger and its winding Snake Road, running along the Kings River. With a name like that, it was a shoo-in to be the area's local haunted hot spot.[1] One of the first to write of the Snake Road specter was Woody Laughnan in *The Fresno Bee's* Halloween edition of 1977: "…and mind you flee the shrieking Witch of [Snake Road] for fear she carry you off into the eerie fog to the cursed badlands beyond the blood-soaked river…"

Years ago, an unnamed mother of two was driving down Snake Road with her two young daughters just a little too quickly. When she took a curve too fast, she flew off the road and crashed right into Kings River. Though she fought and struggled to get her seatbelt undone, she couldn't in time, and therefore she drowned. As for her daughters, they were old enough to get free of the car somehow and make it about a mile downstream before they eventually drowned as well.

F-11   Kings River Canyon Highway, Fresno County, California

PHOTO BY "DICK" WHITTINGTON

Kings River, La Llorona's most famous haunt in California.

Since that day, La Llorona-like tales of a woman in white walking up and down the windy road have emerged. All the while, she calls out for her missing children and will flag down any motorist to ask if they have seen them as well. If anything, it seems as though someone retrofitted the La Llorona story to take place on Snake Road. If you'll recall, La Llorona typically had two children, as was the case in this account. And instead of making it a story warning against affairs, premarital pregnancies, unwanted children, etc.; it was a cautionary tale to keep drivers from going too fast along the curvy road, the

maximum suggested speed of which is 25 miles per hour. However, an alternative stated that a car coming from the other direction ran into the mother and a single daughter. Only the daughter was killed in the accident, and the careless driver fled into the woods. The enraged mother followed the driver and was never seen again… except in her ghostly form where she hunts her daughter's killer.

Interestingly, some referred to her as "la Senorita Lloron" instead of La Llorona. This iteration pre-dated the version with the car and was more traditional, stating that a woman was trying to escape an abusive husband with her two children. They left their home in a deep fog and the woman lost sight of them, never to be seen again. Thereafter, she wondered if they tumbled into the river and drowned, or if perhaps her angry husband had found them in the fog and taken them.

In the area of Packwood Creek, forty miles away, was this legend, reported on Halloween of 1977 in the *Fresno Bee*:

A long time ago, before the first settlers came, a stranded woman is said to have cut the throats of her sick, hungry, cold and starving children and buried them in a shallow grave beside the creek. A heavy rain storm swept the creek that night, washing away the bodies, and the woman returns, sobbing, shrieking on every wind-driven rain, panic-stricken because she cannot find the graves of her young ones.

However, even that iteration was tied to vehicles. In some cases, she was a "good witch" who would help cars navigate the fog. Although she would appear in a frightening manner by leaping onto the hood of the car, she would then begin helping the terrified driver navigate the deadly fog. In other cases, she was a bad witch, and if a car stopped, she might steal the children from within it.

If anything, the La Llorona-like wraith of California proves that the legend is adaptable and certainly here to stay.

Chapter Notes

[1] Technically it's called Channel Road, but due to many winding curves it has been nicknamed Snake Road.

PART III

HER KITH & KIN

Que viene el Coco.

Francisco de Goya's "Here Comes the Boogeyman" c.1797.

EL LLORÓN

THE CRYING MAN OF DURANGO

It probably shouldn't come as a surprise that La Llorona has a male counterpart in the form of El Llorón. It should also come as no surprise that the one to resurrect the ghost from the recesses of folklore was J. Frank Dobie. During one of his Mexican sojourns, Dobie heard the tale of a father who wailed for his dead wife and child every October from fellow writer Everardo Gámez.

Gámez collected the story himself while vacationing at the Rancho de Alemán in Durango on October 15, 1905. The author of the tale was doing some late-night writing in a little hut of an abandoned settlement called Los Hornitos. Meaning the little ovens, the place used to be a Spanish settlement populated by small furnaces used to melt various metals from local mining ventures. At about eight o'clock, some woodcutters burst into Gámez's room in fear. All were crossing themselves while others began to pray.

"What passes?" Gámez asked.

"Hear, hear you. It is El Llorón," one of the men answered.

Familiar with the old wives' tale of Durango's Crying Man, Gámez dismissed it as the howling of dogs, but an elderly man among the group staunchly disagreed. "No senor," he said. "It is the Crying Man. Listen, listen yourself. This comes about inevitably on this very day each year."[1]

Gámez challenged the men to step outside into the darkness with him to pinpoint the noise, still certain it was a mournful dog. The men relented, and no source of the noise, ghostly nor animal, was found that night. Upon returning to the hut, the old timer proceeded to tell the story of El Llorón.

Depiction of Hidalgo's siege of the Alhóndiga de Granaditas in Guanajuato on September 28, 1810, by José Díaz del Castillo, c.1910.

The backdrop for El Llorón's origin was the Mexican War of Independence, wherein the Mexican people won freedom from the Spanish empire in 1821. The tale of El Llorón was set in the early days of the war in 1812. El Llorón, when he was still human, was a Spanish smelter in the region of Los Hornitos. He had a home in the region with a beautiful wife and newborn daughter. He had also accumulated considerable wealth in the form of silver bars and coins. Fearing that he would lose his wealth in the instability, but also knowing he could not transport it with him, he elected to hide his treasure and come back for it after the war was over.

To help him bury so much gold, the rich Spaniard utilized his poor man servant in the task. This man also had a wife and one child, about the same age as his master's. The servant's wife was no fool. She was well-aware that rich men would often kill anyone who knew the location of their buried wealth. Fearing her husband would be killed, the servant's wife went to the wife of the Spaniard, knowing her to have been good-hearted and compassionate in the past.

A representation of mestizos in a "Caste Painting" from the colonial era, c.1870.

As the servant girl had hoped, the wife was indeed sympathetic to her cause. Not wanting her husband to murder his servant, she literally put herself in the shoes of the servant's wife. As it was, she knew if the Indian servant woman went to plead for her husband's life, then the Spaniard might kill the wife in addition to the husband. In an effort to make her husband relate to his servant, she decided to don the attire of the Indian servant's wife. In her mind, upon seeing her dressed as the servant woman, perhaps the husband might sympathize and spare the man's life.

The wife walked to the treasure's secret burial spot carrying their little daughter in her arms to further the point that he would make an orphan out of the servant's daughter. The wife was too late, though, and stumbled upon the horrific scene of her husband beheading the body of the already dead servant. She was too shocked to even illicit a scream and watched in silent horror as her husband rolled the servant's corpse into its grave.

Dobie's wife, Bertha, who translated the tale, noted that it may have derived from a similar fable from Mexico City. In that one, a greedy Spaniard had killed his brother to gain possession of a joint tract of land that both owned. After killing his sibling, the Spaniard commanded his slave to take care of his sister-in-law and his little niece, instructing him to murder them and then brick them up inside the house behind a wall. The slave did as commanded, not knowing that who he killed was actually his master's wife and child, who had just arrived unexpectedly from Spain.

The Spaniard looked up and saw who he assumed to be the Indian's wife watching him from a distance. Either taking out a pistol or dashing up to her—the story isn't specific as to how—the Spaniard "aimed a blow at the head of the woman," killing her instantly. He rolled the woman's corpse into the pit to join her husband, then turned his attention to the little infant that she had dropped. The wailing baby girl had landed in a heap of upturned soil from the grave.

"And this child, why should she live and what could I do with her?" the cruel Spaniard mused.[2] Fearing her very existence might lead to the scene of the crime, the Spaniard kicked his own daughter into the pit to join her mother and buried her alive. Dawn was approaching by the time he had finished covering up his crime, and a "scud of rosy cloud was announcing the day of blood."[3]

It was at that moment that a feeling of dread began to creep over him, as though something wasn't right with his own wife and daughter. Speedily, he proceeded on home to find the very woman whom he thought he had just murdered waiting.

"What is the meaning of this?" the Spaniard asked the servant woman, who responded that she was awaiting the return of his wife, who went to beg for her own husband's life.

"Heavens! What have I done?" the man cried out in desperation. He fled back to the scene of the crime and spent the entire night groaning and wailing over his evil deeds. The next morning, locals found the man dead, hanging from an oak tree with a noose around his neck. The man had taken his own life to end his suffering, only like La Llorona, the powers of Heaven would not allow him eternal rest and peace. That is why, every night on the anniversary of his hideous crime, El Llorón was sentenced to wander the blood-soaked earth of Los Hornitos.

Chapter Notes

---

[1] Dobie, *Puro Mexicano*, p.170.
[2] Ibid, p.172.
[3] Ibid, p.173.

VAMPIRE WOMEN
OF TLAXCALA

TALES OF THE TLAHUELPUCHI

I f you lived in rural Mexico in the mid-1950s, chances are the local boogey-woman wasn't La Llorona, but the vampiric child-killer the tlahuelpuchi. And unlike La Llorona, the tlahuelpuchi had a documented body count. Infant death in the night was so widespread in the state of Tlaxcala that it prompted a government investigation. It came to the attention of the authorities when an alarming number of infant death certificates listed the cause of death as "*chupado por la bruja*," or "sucked by the witch." The babies in question almost always died at night and were found with severe bruising or discoloration on their upper bodies. State authorities were sent to the capital city of the region, Tlaxcala City, to get to the bottom of the mystery.

Suspicious of the death certificates—and unable to prove whether or not vampiric witches were indeed responsible—by 1954 the Mexican government decreed that any death certificate citing "*chupado por la bruja*" as the cause of death would be subject to an investigation. The government assumed that negligence was to blame rather than the supernatural and hoped the fear of repercussions might curb the alarming rate of infant deaths. Did the ploy work? That's hard to say. Residents ceased listing "*chupado por la bruja*" as the cause of death most likely to keep the government out of their towns and villages, but the deaths still continued off and on in the region into the next decade.

Tlaxcala region of Mexico on a map.

Tlaxcala is one of the smaller rural states of Central Mexico. The name itself dates all the way back to the pre-Conquest era in the form of a kingdom named Tlaxcala that had never formally joined the Aztec Empire despite sharing the same language and customs. The legend of the vampire witch, or Tlahuelpuchi, dated back to these times. The legend was unique to the area and didn't extend far outside of its confines. The myth always told of a shape-shifting vampire which subsisted on the blood of young infants, typically between two to ten months of age because the blood of a child that age was the most invigorating to them. The myth of the tlahuelpuchi was quite different from that of a typical vampire because certain women were born as a tlahuelpuchi—there was no occult ritual or vampire bite to transform them.[1]

The curse of the tlahuelpuchi was said to be irreversible and the girl in question would not even know that she was a vampire until puberty. Upon the tragic realization, the girl's soul would be lost for several days as she became infused with special powers. It was said that the witch's family was usually aware of her affliction and kept it a secret since they believed the transformation was no fault of their own. However, there was another reason they wouldn't reveal or kill a tlahuelpuchi within their family. If they did, they themselves might turn into a vampire. By the same token, the tlahuelpuchi was incapable of killing their blood relatives or even relatives by marriage. Like La Llorona, these vampiric specters were lone wolves. The tlahuelpuchi did not socialize or form covens with other witches and kept to themselves.

The powers of the tlahuelpuchi included the ability to shapeshift into various animals, usually birds of some kind similar to the bird-like Lilin. Some tlahuelpuchi could even transform into tiny insects to crawl their way through a keyhole and gain access to a home. The most common form they took was that of a turkey, which generated a supernatural glow. Actually, the glow was where the specter derived its name, coming from the Aztec word *tlahuia* "to illuminate," thus tlahuelpuchi. Perhaps tying into its luminescence were reports that the tlahuelpuchi could also transform into fireballs, a common facet of witch folklore across the southwestern U.S. In addition to the glow as a tell-tale sign, the animal or person in question might also smell of blood, albeit faintly.

Though the turkey was the most common animal form for the witch, it occasionally took on other forms depending on the witch's goal at the time. If she had a long way to go, she would certainly choose a bird capable of flight, like a crow or buzzard. But, if her house call was only a short distance, she might only transform into a cat or coyote. However, she always had to shapeshift into a bird of some sort when it came time to feed. To keep the parents or older siblings asleep, she would emit a supernatural mist that made certain they would not awaken as she fed. To do so, she sucked the baby's blood through a long, needle-like tongue. Upon finishing, she would often leave the body outside of the crib or away from the sleeping mat.

Supposedly, shamans and medicine men were the only ones able to resist the witch's sleep mist. However, if one awakened and managed to ward off the witch, it was said she would return in the daylight hours to enact her revenge. At the very worst, she might put a spell on her prey that caused them to do self-harm, such as marching off a cliff. In less extreme cases, she might have transformed into a coyote or other predatory animal to kill a family's livestock or transform into a donkey to simply ruin newly planted crops.

The witch's method of transformation was quite elaborate. On the last Saturday of the month, she had to build a fire of dry zoapotl leaves, capulin wood, copal, and agave roots in her kitchen. While chanting, she would walk across the fire in the shape of a cross, north-south/east-west, three times before sitting on the fire facing north, which enabled her to enact the transformation. To reduce her size to that of the animal she wished to emulate, she would remove her legs.[2]

After turning into a bird of flight, her legs sat in the kitchen. When she returned home, she would sit on the fire again and fit her legs back onto her body. However, after many years of this ritual, the witch would begin to look lopsided and walk with a limp. As such, unfortunately, elderly women who suffered naturally from these conditions were falsely labeled as witches in many cases. Other unfair correlations were made between the tlahuelpuchi and being obese, thinking that a woman had become overweight from consuming too much blood. And in traditional witch fashion, some elderly women were stereotyped as a tlahuelpuchi simply because they had long noses, squinty eyes, and squeaky voices.

As to other specific details concerning the tlahuelpuchi's habits, they were said to be most active during the coldest, wettest months of the year. In the summer, they fed during the rainy season, while in the winter, they attacked on the coldest nights. Some experts cited December, January, February, June, July, and August as the most common months due to the cold and rain, respectively. (However, from a practical perspective, these are also the nights most likely for an infant to freeze to death.) In terms of when the vampires attacked, anywhere between the hours of 12:00-3:00 AM were the most common. However, they did not require feeding every night and supposedly only fed a few days out of the month. Furthermore, though rare, they occasionally attacked non-infants, like older children and adults, out of desperation, it was said. If they went without feeding altogether for one month, they would die. They would also die if they did not feed by daybreak when in their shapeshifted form.

Sanctuary of Ocotlan, Tlaxcala.

The infant victims of the tlahuelpuchi required special funerals, usually seen over by a folk healer or priest with experience in warding off supernatural evil. Unlike other funerals, no music would be played, and a cross made of pine ashes would be placed under the casket. After the burial, nearly all traces of the child were wiped clean. Their clothes were burned, no flowers were ever placed on their graves, and the child wouldn't even be remembered on the Day of the Dead.

Warding off a tlahuelpuchi wasn't completely dissimilar to a European vampire, as garlic was suggested in some cases, along with adorning the crib with Christian iconography and symbols. Though, being in Mexico, interestingly enough, the practitioners wrapped the garlic—and sometimes onions—in a tortilla. As for religious symbols, some parents put clothespins in the shape of a cross. Typically, though, the best way to protect a baby was to put a mirror in its crib as the tlahuelpuchi abhorred mirrors and would shun them.

One of the more well-documented cases of a tlahuelpuchi occurred on December 8, 1960, again in the state of Tlaxcala. Specifically, it occurred in San Pedro Xolotla, a rural community in the vicinity of La Malintzi volcano. It was said to occur on an unusually cold night. Though several families were hit by the tlahuelpuchi that night, the most documentation afforded to a couple identified only as Filemón and Francisca, who lived in the home of Filemón's parents with their four children. They were in their early thirties, were primarily weavers, and had been working late carding wool and making yarn. Before turning in, Francisca breastfed her seven-month-old, Cristina, then put her on her sleeping mat for the night. Three hours later, Francisca awoke to a terrifying sight. A bright light was floating outside of her window. Similar to earlier reports of the tlahuelpuchi's ability to emit a sleep-inducing mist, try as she might, Francisca could not make herself get out of bed. Her body felt tired and heavy and so she fell asleep. Soon she woke again to find a mist filling her room and out of it formed a blue and red colored bird-like creature, said to resemble a chicken. That was her last memory before passing out again.

The next morning at 6 AM, Filemón found baby Cristina dead. Not only that, she had been moved from her sleeping pad to the middle of the floor. As was typical with reports of the tlahuelpuchi, her chest and neck region were mottled and purplish in color, and her torso was covered in scratches. That same morning, six other dead infants were found across the village, making for seven in total. Was it the tlahuelpuchi, or just the bitter cold that killed the babies? Though the latter seems more likely, why then did nearly all of the mothers report the same state of sleep paralyses? Were they ashamed that their babies froze to death in the night and used the tlahuelpuchi as an excuse, or did the shape-shifting witch actually pay them a visit?

Warding off witches in Hispanic folklore often required a bizarre rigmarole where one might turn their clothes inside out to reflect bad energy back at the witch. In a similar vein, to ward off a tlahuelpuchi, one might take off their pants, turn one leg inside out, and then throw the pants at the tlahuelpuchi. The other method, equally strange, was to place a rock within a white handkerchief and throw it at the witch. Lastly, if one was wearing a hat, they could remove it, place it upside down on the floor, and then drive a knife through it. Any of these three methods would immobilize the creature, and afterward, it could be dispatched permanently. When it came down to actually destroying a tlahuelpuchi for good, a stake might be driven through the heart or the witch could simply be decapitated. The only truly unique method of killing one of these vampires was to find their disembodied legs at the site of their kitchen fire and destroy them.

All that said, those methods were folkloric, and the only historically reported executions of a tlahuelpuchi consisted of the accused being stoned or clubbed to death. Afterward, the accused witch's corpse was tossed into a ravine. According to Robert Bitto of Mexico Unexplained, "many women in Tlaxcala have been killed for being suspected tlahuelpuchis."[3] As far as anyone knows, the last known execution of a tlahuelpuchi occurred in 1973.

Chapter Notes

---

[1] There can also be male tlahuelpuchi but they are very rare.

[2] Folklore said that they did this because, by removing their legs and losing the ability to walk upright, they lost what made them human— perhaps drawing a parallel to the serpent in the garden forced to crawl upon its belly after tempting Adam and Eve.

[3] Bitto, "The Vampire Witches of Central Mexico," Mexico Unexplained. https://mexicounexplained.com/vampire-witches-central-mexico/

WHAT MAKES A MONSTER? One of Sheriff Joe Wilson's deputies agreed to pose for The Tribune in the costume believed to be worn by the "South Valley Monster" during his visits. The garb includes black long johns, a white mask and a black wig. The hooves he is holding are believed to be responsible for the prints found after the monster visits.

Albuquerque Tribune (October 28, 1966).

SOUTH VALLEY SPECTER
THE CRY-BABY MONSTER

In mid-October of 1966, a strange La Llorona-like specter stalked the South Valley, a rural suburb of Albuquerque in Bernalillo County. Settled by Spanish and Mexican families over 400 years ago, the beautiful valley was lined with irrigation ditches linked to the Rio Grande. As it was, the decade of the 1960s was the South Valley's last hurrah as a rural farming community untainted by the more urban lifestyle of the encroaching metropolis to the north. Slowly but surely, Albuquerque stretched itself into the confines of the valley in search of more land for urban housing. And, as alluded to above, in addition to encroaching economic development, the South Valley also fell prey to something more sinister in the 1960s. In the fall months, a strange specter began prowling the neighborhoods near the Rio Grande. It was described as a man-like creature with a black body and a pure white face devoid of any features. Given several names, it was best-known as the "Faceless Monster" for reasons just given, and also the "Crybaby Monster" due to the fact that it was often heard crying like a baby.

The *Albuquerque Journal* and *Albuquerque Tribune* loved it, naturally. Both the *Journal* and the *Tribune* broke the story in separate articles on October 14th chronicling events from the night before. Though it wasn't the first night that the fiend made its appearance on the property of the Clifford McGuire residence, it was apparently the first time that the police came to investigate. And where the police go, the press will follow.

The *Albuquerque Tribune* reported that the family had a run in with something that "looks like a man, runs like an animal and cries like a baby." This description was made by 19-year-old C.D. McGuire, who described his encounter with the "thing" as "hair raising." Though no initial date was given, in the *Tribune's* article of the 14th, the family said that "the thing" had been appearing "almost nightly" on their property, while the *Journal's* article of the same day stated that the being had been prowling around their residence for three weeks, meaning that it would have begun its reign of terror in late September.

'Monster' Cries Like Baby

Hairy, Blank-Faced 'Something' Reported Roaming in South Valley

By ERNIE HELTSLEY

Albuquerque Journal (October 14, 1966).

During the first encounter, C.D. confronted the figure and it hit him in the chest, knocking him unconscious. When he awoke, C.D. found hoof-like tracks in the ground. In the ensuing weeks, whenever the "thing" would return, C.D.'s chest would begin to hurt. Also heralding the monster's appearance was the fact that the family's radio would stop playing. Then the McGuires would hear scratching along the walls followed by a strange wail that sounded like a crying baby. The *Journal* of the 14th elaborated, "McGuire's children are afraid to sleep in their back bedroom..." and it elaborated that "every time the older son hears it 'cry like a baby' his chest begins hurting all over again where the monster reportedly hit him." The article continued that the officers had seen the "fork-like marks and heard the story several times." Clifford McGuire added that he didn't report the incident before then because he thought "people would think we were crazy.'"

After the story's publication, other witnesses came forth to reveal past sightings. According to a caller who didn't wish to be identified, the same monster was seen haunting the Old Town Bridge in either 1939, 1940, or 1941—they couldn't remember. Specifically, they said that "the same monster type story" was circulated and the caller told the *Tribune*, "I know a witness to that sighting who has told us about it many times." The woman continued that, "I suggested that he call the paper but he said that he didn't want to scare anybody." The paper continued that, "The descriptions of the 25-year-old monster and last night's creature are much the same, the caller said."

Image of Albuquerque at about the era that this story took place.

As usual, descriptions of the monster varied in the days to come. A witness in the Northeast Heights region, Jerry Goldstein, reported seeing the monster in a *Tribune* article entitled "Monster in Heights". It stated that he saw a "black furry creature" with a white face standing six feet tall as opposed to five. The paper also specified that the "creature" had two legs, or in other words, it was bipedal like a human being. Nothing terribly dramatic happened and Goldstein simply observed it easily jump over a high block fence, badly scaring a yellow cat in the process. Perhaps the oddest thing about the encounter was that it took place at 9:30 in the morning rather than at night. The same article reported a much

Monster Heard But Not Seen

The so-called monster was heard but not seen in the vicinity of Jeanette and Wilshire SW Saturday night, it was reported to the sheriff's office.

Officers said the area is near the home of Clifford McGuire, 415 Wilshire SW, who first reported seeing the creature two days ago.

Police and the sheriff's office reported two other sightings — one in Northeast Heights and the other north of Central just west of the Rio Grande. Both are considerable distances from Wilshire SW.

Albuquerque Journal (October 16, 1966).

more interesting encounter from Frank Trujillo, a 29-year-old with a ranch in the area. Trujillo stated he was returning home from the ranch at 1 A.M. when he saw "a dark, hairy object by the car window" about five feet tall, and "that it tried to grab him when he got out of the car..." The article was unfortunately vague on the details, and the next paragraph stated that Trujillo tried to get a gun from inside his home and when he returned outside, the creature was long gone.

At noon the following day, another area rancher, 20-year-old Tom Bizzell, heard his horses making an unusual racket in their corral. When he went to investigate, he found that the horses had kicked down some boards in a panicked attempt to get out of the corral. Likewise, his dogs were in the corral "where they don't usually go."

The article's concluding paragraph stated, "He said he found footprints of three-finger or toe type. Two toes are close together and the other is at the side." Earlier in the article, it was also implied that the monster's abode had been discovered, though this point was never followed up on, unless the paper was hinting that the creature lived in the vicinity of the two ranches.

By the 17th a frenzy had been worked up over the incident. Similar to the case of the Zodiac killer, the "monster" began calling people on the telephone. In the *Tribune's* piece on the 17th, "'Monster' Stories Grow; Some Laugh, Others Fear," it reported, "The latest development is a rash of telephone calls from the thing. City police reported today more than 100 calls throughout the weekend from people who have been visited by the thing or who have had phone calls from it." The police said that the callers had received threats of "various violences." Naturally, these were all prank calls, though.

An Abominable Cow?

Image of the monster's footprint as it appeared in the
Albuquerque Tribune of October 22, 1966.

Earlier, on Saturday the 15th, an exciting new development occurred. Sheriff Joe Wilson told the press that his deputies had spoken to two men who had witnessed a young man dressed in black pants and a "black bulky sweater" with a "stocking over his face" as he prowled through the yard of none other than Clifford McGuire. The two men confronted the prowler, who they estimated to be 5' 7", and chased him over a fence. Ultimately, the man escaped across an irrigation ditch.

Likewise, the *Journal* of the 16th reported in "Monster Heard But Not Seen" that "The so-called monster was heard but not seen in the vicinity of Jeanette and Wilshire SW Saturday night, it was reported to the sheriff's office." The article noted that the area was near the McGuire home where the monster was most often seen but also added: "Police and the sheriff's office reported two other sightings — one in Northeast Heights and the other north of Central just west of the Rio Grande. Both are considerable distances from Wilshire SW."

On Tuesday of the following week, several copycat or prankster incidents occurred. One boy, pretending to be a monster, jumped from a hiding place, and the girl panicked so much that she ran into a tree. Elsewhere, a woman believed that the thing had kicked in her backdoor and put a dent in it. "Tennis shoe tracks were found nearby," the paper reported.

What may have been the only real monster account came from children, which the paper brushed off: "Children, obviously with big imaginations called the sheriff's office about a 'hairy black monster' twice, once in the 1100 block of Pear SW and another at 2200 block of Rosindo Garcia SW."

On Saturday, October 22nd, a report came in that the monster scared the family cat of the Willie Baca family in the South Valley so badly that it could no longer meow. Notably, the strange "baby's cry" was reported again in this instance. The story ended with a quote from one of the deputies regarding the noise: "They (Baca and his family) all heard him cryin'. They said it was the most horrible cry—like a baby. It shook Willie, too. And the cat was so scared he couldn't even meow." Before closing, the same article also stated that calls on the monster were finally starting to dwindle.

And indeed, the monster's newspaper trail died down in late October and was by then the butt of jokes. One article was headlined "Valley Monster to be at Party" (published October 26th in the *Tribune*) and promised that a reenactor of the monster would be at the Boys Club Halloween Party.

The October 28th edition of the *Tribune* sounded the monster's death knell. It reported how the previous evening the police responded to a burglary in progress in the South Valley at about 9:30. The paper stated that the deputies spotted the monster fleeing the scene and chased it to a barn two blocks away. Inside the barn was found the monster's discarded clothes in the form of "a pair of faded black long johns, a wiry black wig, a whiteface mask, (homemade variety with cut out slant eyes), and two elk hooves."[1]

The paper noted that "the hooves could have been used to make the prints" found previously. In true Scooby Doo fashion, the *Journal* speculated that the hooves could have been used to hit young C.D. McGuire several weeks back as well. As for the suspect, he was described as being a skinny, small 22-year-old identified only as "Jim," the last name purposefully withheld and the first given out only by accident.

And that is where the paper trail ended. However, while it may seem like a simple matter of 'case closed,' there are still too many supernatural threads dangling to brush it off entirely. How the hoaxer would have generated the strange infant-like cry that so many witnesses reported is puzzling. And, while skeptics could argue that C.D. McGuire's chest pains upon hearing the wailing were psychologically induced, the radio interference that occurred every time the monster wailed warrants further explanation.[2] As such, it's a viable theory that, in the beginning, perhaps a real supernatural entity was stalking the South Valley. Then, as interest in the ghost grew, a hoaxer took to imitating it and was caught by the police.

The specter's white face, crying noises, and close association with the Rio Grande arguably liken it to La Llorona, or perhaps El Llorón, since the specter was always identified as male. Variations of La Llorona had her dressed in all black with a white, featureless face, just like the South Valley Specter. *Tales of Witchcraft and the Supernatural in the Pecos Valley* presented one such story in the account "It Didn't Have a Face." The sighting occurred either in the 1910s or early 1920s. The witness, from Sena, New Mexico, said that "[La Llorona] didn't have a face." He elaborated that "perhaps it was wearing something to cover her face."[3]

Whether the South Valley Specter was man or monster, it's odd that La Llorona wasn't mentioned in any of the articles considering the similarities between the two criers. On that note, it's entirely possible that the suspect was trying to portray

La Llorona the entire time and the papers never picked up on it. Or, bearing that explanation, maybe it really was the Wailing Woman all along...

Chapter Notes

---

[1] The black wig could have been an attempt to emulate La Llorona's long black hair. The elk-hooves could have been a nod to La Llorona's animal traits more often found in the bordering state of Texas.

[2] If one wanted to speculate that the perpetrator was carrying around a portable noise making device that produced the baby calls and interfered with the family radio signal, that could be a good theory except that such things were not widely available to the general public in 1966. As an aside, and another can of worms entirely, the papers were also reporting UFO sightings over Albuquerque at the same time the monster was being sighted.

[3] Garcia, *Tales of Witchcraft*, p.121.

15

PAVLA BLANCA

WHITE LADY OF WHITE SANDS

One of the more popular ghost legends of White Sands National Monument is tangent to La Llorona, involving a ghostly white female specter. It is the Lady of the Sands, alternately known as Pavla Blanca, which basically translates to *white dust*. So the story goes, every night, she can be seen in her white wedding gown, searching for her lost lover along the sands. Others say the winds and heavy breezes whip up white sand into the air over the dunes, giving the illusion of the beautiful figure in her wedding dress. Roswell writer Will Robinson wrote of a trip to White Sands along with Pedro Cassini in the 1930s:

> One evening old Pedro was counting his beads as the sun set in a burst of glory over the San Andreas Mountains. "The White Lady will rise again when the moon comes over the Sacramentos," he said. "Twice it will be for me. Once more will be the last, as it was with my father and many others who have seen her."
>
> The wind was coming across the plains of the Sacramentos from the southwest in long, steady flows, but not so very hard. Most likely it bounced off the prairies at times, and when it struck it moved things.
>
> "There she is," said one of the men pointing to the top of one of the great dunes. Here the wind seemed to be deflected, and high in the air rose a spiral of white, light

enough for the mountains to be seen through it, but positive enough that there was no mistaking that the White Lady was walking again in the vast area of alabaster covering 270 square miles. Old Pedro continued to count his beads until the White Lady gathered her fleecy garments about her and vanished into the night.

I never again saw the White Lady though the years of patrol the eyes were always alert to see her. It is not often that she comes, and the primitives are glad of it. She is lovely, but no man or woman can see her but three times and live.[1]

White Sands. (Historical Society for Southeast New Mexico)

Bula Charles wrote of seeing the ghost with her husband, Tom, at White Sands in her booklet, *Tales of the Tularosa*, too.

...in the midst of the silence, the wind breathed. I could hear it sighing across the sand. I could feel it, half-hot, half-cool. A swirling eddy swept up a long slope off to the left, like a dust devil on a hot day. But it wasn't like a dust devil.

"Look." Tom was pointing. "Pavla Blanca."

The eddy took shape as it neared the summit of the dune; it filled out—it was a woman. Right at the crest she stood erect and bent forward, as if peering into the shadows beyond the hill upon which she stood. Pavla Blanca, the White Wraith, dressed in her flowing wedding gown. She poised for an instant, still looking, then ran along the rippled edge of the dune. She disappeared with a sound that was halfway between a sigh and a sob. Of course it was just the wind. But I decided, from that time on, to leave it to others to refute old Spanish legends.[2]

The real identity of Pavla Blanca was the fiancé of a conquistador. Her name was Mañuela, and the conquistador was Hernando de Luna, one of Francisco de Coronado's men employed in the search for the fabled Seven Cities of Gold. Mañuela remained in Mexico under the agreement that when the northern Kingdom of New Spain was properly settled, de Luna would send for her to join him. Instead, on the trek across the dreaded Jornada del Muerto, Coronado's men were attacked by the Apache. De Luna became separated from the troop and soon found himself lost among the blinding white sands. Coronado and his men traced de Luna's tracks across the dunes but never found his body. It was as though he disappeared into thin air.

Mañuela headed north into the region upon news of her fiancé's disappearance, escorted by a group of Jesuits. One night, under cover of darkness, Mañuela donned her wedding dress, mounted a horse, and rode off into the sands, never to be seen again—not in corporeal form, at least. As stated before, now her ghostly essence is seen among the swirling sands carried in the winds.

Either history repeated itself years later, or the tale of Pavla Blanca received an update in modern times. Writer Alice Bullock related the tale of two young lovers, an Alamogordo teacher and her fiancé, who went for a romantic picnic on the sands one evening before sunset. The man, who was not native to the area, was fascinated by the dunes. After dinner, as his fiancé packed up the picnic baskets, he decided to climb the tallest dune he saw. The teacher watched as a strange wind erased his footsteps from the sand. As she called to him to come back, he was completely obscured by the sandy winds. When they subsided, he was gone, never to be seen again.

White Sands. (Historical Society for Southeast New Mexico)

Supposedly, search parties scoured the sands only to find nothing.[3] Bullock stated that the teacher herself disappeared into the sands in search of her beloved. She was apparently destined to become another woman in white, forevermore to be seen wearing her wedding dress, dancing atop the dunes as the white sand swirls around her for eternity.

Chapter Notes

[1] Robinson, "The White Lady of the Sands," *Yucca Land*, p.193.
[2] Charles, *Tales of the Tularosa*, pp. 50-51.
[3] No stories about the incident can be found in newspapers, alluding to this just being an urban legend.

THE DONKEY LADY
OF SAN ANTONIO

BEAST-WOMAN OF BEXAR COUNTY

Although she likely began as an offshoot of La Llorona, the Donkey Lady of San Antonio has undeniably carved out her own niche in Texas folklore. As a testament to this is the fact that she's actually called the Donkey Lady and not La Llorona. Therefore, one could argue that she's become her own distinct entity. In the words of *Weird Texas* authors Mark Sceurman and Mark Moran, "Anyone who has gone to school in San Antonio has heard of the Donkey Lady."[1]

Like Woman Hollering Creek, the specter even has her own placename in the form of Donkey Lady Bridge located about thirty miles southwest of San Antonio. As opposed to La Llorona's wailing and weeping, the Donkey Lady is frequently heard snorting around in the bushes and is sometimes at first thought to be an animal. But, when a witness looks at her, they will see a woman with a donkey's head, hence the name. Encounters with the Donkey Lady are arguably more intense than those with the Wailing Woman, as one account had her leaping onto the hood of a pickup truck and snarling at the driver and his passengers.[2] A similar story, taking place in 1987, had some young people trying to summon the specter of Donkey Lady Bridge by honking their horn on the overpass. As in the other account, the result was a damaged car and a smashed-in windshield.

As to how the Donkey Lady came to be, like La Llorona, she had multiple origin stories and dead children figured into them to a lesser extent. The most basic account went that a long time ago, a farmer, his wife, and their children led a peaceful existence in the country outside of San Antonio. For reasons unknown, the farmer decided to murder his family, setting fire to the home. His children perished, but his wife survived, only terribly disfigured. Her hands had melted into stumps resembling hooves, and her face now resembled a donkey. Forever bereaved, she took to living in the wilderness and terrorizing anyone in the vicinity. Some say this incident occurred in the 1950s, while others dated it back to the Old West.

A variant decided to mix an actual donkey into the tale. In it, a cruel stranger had come to the farmhouse of the happy family. For his own deranged amusement, the stranger began to beat the family's donkey, and so they chased him away. He returned later that night to set their house on fire. Amidst the chaos, the mother burst out of the house, screaming as her body burned. She chased the arsonist away from the scene and eventually leaped into the creek, though her body was never found.

A story with even more vague origins alleged that the Donkey Lady was a kindly woman who made a living raising donkeys. One day, one of her donkeys bit the son of a prominent San Antonio family. In anger, the members of the family ambushed the woman when she was walking one of her donkeys along the bridge. Killing the woman and her pet, both were tossed into the creek and somehow combined into the fearsome Donkey Lady. Yet another story utilized and infused elements of the previous two, having the visitor to the farm being a well-to-do man who was bitten by the family donkey. As in the other tales, the family ran him off and he returned with members of his family to set their house on fire.

Though she has yet to stray to other areas across the U.S. as La Llorona has done, the Donkey Lady of San Antonio has certainly carved a niche for herself among the specters of the Southwest.

Chapter Notes

---

[1] Sceurman & Moran, *Weird Texas*, p.19.

[2] The teller of the tale, identified as Tim Stevens in *Weird Texas*, heard the story firsthand from the witness who showed Stevens the damage done to the truck in the story.

LA LLORONA, THE DONKEY LADY, & THE CHURCH

S everal origin stories for both La Llorona and the Donkey Lady were infused with religious overtones and served as warnings against betraying the church in some way or another. From *When Darkness Falls: Tales of San Antonio Ghosts and Hauntings* came an origin story for the Donkey Lady that hinged heavily upon the Catholic Church. In it, a young woman had just been married in a beautiful church in Mexico. At the altar, she promised the priest performing the ceremony that she would give her firstborn son to the priesthood. However, when the day came and she gave birth to a son, she could not stand to give him up. As a consequence, her house later caught fire, burning up her children and deforming her own face so that it took on the characteristics of a donkey. This is how the Donkey Lady of San Antonio came to be.[1]

Several of La Llorona's origin stories had particularly strong religious themes as well. One had La Llorona as the mother of twin girls who, because of being identical, had a mishap during their baptism. One of the girls was baptized twice, and the other not at all. This was a bad omen. When the unbaptized baby matured into womanhood, she had two children of her own. She did not love them, and so drowned them in an acequia. When she later died herself, God sentenced her to roam the earth until she had recovered her drowned children. While her not being baptized as a baby probably shouldn't have affected the outcome of the story, it was an interesting flourish, nonetheless. Another account, from the abandoned mining town of Dawson, New Mexico, had La Llorona as the mother of an unbaptized baby who haunted the local church as a skeleton woman.

Another overtly religious origin story for La Llorona had her more or less punished by the Virgin Mary. The account, taken from a Las Vegas old-timer, stated that La Llorona originated at the time of Christ. "They believe that when Christ was being persecuted, mothers gave up their sons to go fight for him. There was one woman who couldn't see why so many lives should be sacrificed for one and she was always crying for him. People would try to console her but she'd say that for her there was no consolation so our Blessed Mother told her she would never find consolation and she would walk the earth forever crying because for her there was no consolation."[2]

Section Notes

---

[1] Williams, *When Darkness Falls*, pp.296-97.
[2] Robe, *Hispanic Legends from New Mexico*, pp.95-96.

LA SIGUANABA

HORSE-HEADED HORROR

Whereas the Donkey Lady was likely an offshoot of La Llorona, the Wailing Woman herself might have descended from another folkloric specter called Siguanaba, who has so many things in common with La Llorona it's hard to know where to start. That said, Siguanaba never frequented in the American Southwest like La Llorona and the she-specter stuck to Central and South America. She always appeared as a beautiful woman... initially at least. Typically, she was seen near bodies of water. If she wasn't bathing in a river, she might've been washing her clothes at a watering hole. Assuming she wasn't nude, she typically wore a silky black dress. Her favorite target was adulterous men, who she lured into secluded areas of the wilderness. Then, when it was too late to run, her beautiful face turned from that of a woman's to that of a horse's—or a skeleton, depending on the locality.

As we all know, skeletal and horse-headed La Lloronas are many in the Americas. And, also like La Llorona, in addition to targeting men, Siguanaba occasionally lured children into the jungle as well. To do so, she shapeshifted into the form of the child's mother, something she also did with the men from time to time, in that case turning into their wife or girlfriend. Whether child or adult, anyone who wasn't killed by Siguanaba would go mad if nothing else.

https://en.wikipedia.org/wiki/Siuanaba#/media/File:Siguanaba.JPG

"La Siguanaba, Leyenda" by Orlando Callejas c.2008.

Another trait that Siguanaba shares with La Llorona is her origin, which may have stemmed from Spanish settlers in Mexico. In the province of Asturias, there was a legend about the Wagtail, an old hag dressed in black who washed clothes near riverbanks at night. She would transform into a young, beautiful woman and then lead men to their deaths. However, she never sported an equine head. Nonetheless, the idea of a shapeshifting temptress could have been brought to Mexico from Spain. Not that the indigenous residents of Mexico needed any inspiration. They were rife with legends of their own on Naguals, their variety of shapeshifter. Because Naguals often took the form of animals, perhaps a Nagual legend got combined with that of the beautiful but deadly shapeshifter of Spain.

As with La Llorona, the gods of the Aztecs were also in the milieu. According to one legend, the woman who would become Siguanaba was once a beautiful peasant girl, Sihuehuet, who used a combination of her own beauty plus love magic to marry Prince Yeisun. Notably, Yeisun was a demigod, the son of Tlaloc, the rain god. Sihuehuet had a son, Cipitio, with Yeisun, and although she should have been content, when Yeisun went off to war, she cheated on him every chance she got. Eventually, she poisoned Yeisun in an effort to ascend the throne herself. However, the plan backfired, with Yeisun turning into a giant monster and Tlaloc cursed Sihuehuet into Siguanaba, who would at first appear as a beautiful woman until her true, hideous face was revealed. Furthermore, even young Cipitio was cursed to remain a boy forever so that his mother would have to eternally search for him.

As stated before, tales of Siguanaba and her variants are many in Mexico. For instance, in Guatemala, she was associated with gold, often seen with a golden bowl and a golden comb, while in Oaxaca she was known as the jungle witch, Matlazihua. In Mexico City, in many ways she was indistinguishable from La Llorona as she often appeared with a skeletal head like the Wailing Woman. Her origin story, too, was like that of La Llorona's, only further mythologized. Instead of being an ordinary woman, in Mexico City, Siguanaba was the moon goddess and the wife of Tlaloc, who cursed her after her many affairs. If there's one thing in Mexico that differentiated Siguanaba from La Llorona, it was that she only targeted grown men and never children. Therefore, Siguanaba could be considered as a cautionary tale against adultery rather than bad parenting.

In Puebla, she was called Andalona and seemed to have some commonalities with the vampires of nearby Tlaxcala. That's because in Puebla she could fly and had bird-like feet. Mainly she roamed the mountains there as opposed to the rivers and the streams. In Guerrero, she was called the Chaneca, and was once a woman who had an affair with a *chaneque*, which was essentially a duende or magical little person common to folklore the world over. In the state of Durango, she devoured her victims whole at times. The Honduras iteration of Siguanaba, La Cigua, served as a cautionary tale for unbaptized babies. In that case, La Cigua was a beautiful young woman who unfortunately was never baptized, a fact not revealed until she stood at the altar to be married. She never removed her wedding dress as she wandered the countryside forever in mourning.

More tangent to La Llorona is La Sayona, who targeted unfaithful husbands and occasionally had a skeletal face rather than an animal head. Actually, the very name Sayona was a reference to the shawl the woman wore to hide her skeletal face. Native to Venezuela, she was usually found on the roadside asking for a ride. In the car, she would reveal her skeletal face to frighten the driver, sometimes to death. She also appeared to men working in the jungle who were looking to cheat on their wives. In that case, she lured them into the forest as a beautiful woman until she took on some animal form to devour them.

Her most common origin story went that she was once a girl named Casilda who lived in the plains of Venezuela. The most beautiful girl in the small village where she lived, she was happily married to a good man with whom she had a son. One of Casilda's favorite pastimes was swimming nude in the river, far away from the eyes of others—or so she thought. However, a secret admirer often watched her from the bushes. One day, Casilda finally spotted him and yelled for him to leave her alone. The man spoke up and claimed he was there to warn her that her husband was having an affair with her own mother. If he spoke the truth or a lie is uncertain, but Casilda foolishly believed him and set out for her home at once. There she found her husband asleep with their baby son in his arms. Rather than stopping to consider whether the stranger's statement was true or not, she burned their home down in a rage killing her husband and son. After that, it was her mother's turn to suffer. As her husband and son screamed in agony, Casilda picked up a machete and marched to her mother's house. Without even asking if the accusations were true, she stabbed her mother in the stomach. As she lay dying, Casilda's mother cursed her to become La Sayona, whose duty it was to avenge innocent wives who fell victim to adulterous husbands.

Engraving of South American village.

If one encountered any variety of Siguanaba, making the sign of the cross usually could ward her off, although if one wanted to try a more folkloric method, they could bite a machete while rebuking the evil spirit. However, the best method to keep Siguanaba away was to simply be faithful to one's spouse.

LA LECHUZA

OWL WITCH OF MEXICO & TEXAS

Like La Llorona, La Lechuza is another distinctive female specter of the Southwest and Mexico. Not to be confused with witches who simply took the form of owls for their nightly prowls, the Lechuza was more of a were-owl. Or, that is to say, the Lechuza was depicted as a gigantic owl with humanoid features. The Lechuza could be quite large, sometimes standing as tall as seven feet with a fifteen-foot wingspan. Some even claimed that the larger Lechuzas ran cars off the road. And naturally, like all owls, they were seen mostly at night but not always.

La Lechuza's origins usually involved the death of a child in some way or another. Some thought that the original La Lechuza had a child who was wrongly killed by people in her village. A more modern version claimed that her child was killed by a drunk driver, and so, therefore, she was known to attack drunkards. She has also been used as a religious scare tactic similar to La Llorona. For instance, some claimed that the owl witch specifically craved the blood of unbaptized babies. As such, the Lechuza served as an impetus to get one's child baptized at once. La Lechuza could emulate the cries of an infant to lure victims out into the open. And like La Llorona, hearing La Lechuza's cry was considered a bad omen, perhaps foreshadowing that you or someone you know might be about to die.

As stated before, anyone could be at risk of being carried away by La Lechuza, not just children and drunks. However, even if a victim escaped La Lechuza's clutches, if so much as a feather touched them, they would later die. At best, one might only find scratches on their door or windowsill where the Lechuza had tried to gain ingress the night before. Some poured salt along their windowsill to keep La Lechuza out, while another superstition necessitated that one hang a rope with seven knots tied into it over their door.

La Lechuza was not a folktale relegated to encounters from the 19th century, either. In the 1950s, a Lechuza supposedly haunted the border town of Nuevo Laredo. According to Mexico Unexplained and several other sources, the owl-witch was confronted there at an unspecified date. Similar to many witch tales of the previous century, it had the locals luring the Lechuza out of the trees with a young child as bait. When the giant bird-like being appeared, the townsfolk opened fire on it but only managed to hit it in the claw before it got away. The next day, an accused witch living in the town was seen with a crutch and a bandaged leg.

Nuevo Laredo postcard c.1950s.

One of the most prominent waves of Lechuza sightings may have occurred in Texas between 1975 and 1977, where a "Big Bird" was frequently spotted in the Rio Grande region. Reports of a large, bird-like creature with a human face (alternately reported as a man or a woman) began to circulate around Robstown in the Autumn of 1975. The *Corpus Christi Times* of January 22, 1976, ran a story which contained a quote from the Robstown Police Department stating that back in November of 1975, "A bunch of kids fixed them up a dummy of this big bird and hung it in a tree and then called police. We went out there and got it and brought it to the police station."

Detective Daivd Esquivel of the Robstown, Texas, police force inspecting the Lechuza effigy. (Murray Judson photo)

When the sightings jumped into high gear in January of 1976, the Robstown Police Department invited a photographer to see the bird effigy for themselves as though it somehow explained the recent sightings, though it certainly did not. Furthermore, were the police merely assuming this effigy was a prank? It's possible that this Lechuza effigy was, in fact, a serious attempt at either conjuring the witch-monster or perhaps an effort to ward it off.

Man Reports 'Big Bird' Attack

RAYMONDVILLE, Tex. (AP) — A Raymondville man told officers he was attacked by a "big bird" as he stood in the back yard of his home late Wednesday, police said Thursday.

Earlier, several persons in the Lower Rio Grande Valley, including two police officers, reported sighting a large birdlike creature with a wing spread of 10-15 feet, large eyes and a bat-like face.

A spokesman for the Willacy County Sheriff's office said Armando Grimaldo, about 26, told them a big black bird with big eyes and a monkey-like face attacked him and tore his jacket and shirt. The man was taken to a local hospital for treatment and was released after hospital attendants could not find any trace of physical injury.

Grimaldo was at home in bed Thursday, reportedly in shock, and would not discuss the incident with newsmen.

"His wife called us and told us he had been beaten up by a big bird," a city police spokesman said. The officer who went to see Grimaldo said "he was pretty scared and was shaking," a spokesman said.

Neighbors told reporters that Grimaldo told them he was standing in his back yard when he "felt some wind and looked up and this big bird attacked him." The neighbors said they didn't see anything when they went outside after hearing Grimaldo scream.

Abilene Reporter (January 16, 1976).

On the night of January 14, 1976, 26-year-old Armando Grimaldo of Raymondville was attacked by a flying creature when he went outside his mother-in-law's home to smoke a cigarette. In the backyard, Grimaldo suddenly heard a flapping of great wings along with a strange whistle (remember, the Lechuza was said to whistle). Soon he was accosted by the nightmarish flying creature that attempted to carry him away. Its wingspan, he estimated, was in the range of ten to fifteen feet. He described the creature's head as looking like a monkey's or a bat's with no discernable beak. Afterward, he was transported to the Willacy County Hospital in a state of shock.

Mexico Unexplained also related that a Lechuza was seen in Texas the following year in 1977. The incident occurred in Santa Rosa, which is also situated near the border. A woman there claimed to see a huge bird in a tree with a face like an old woman's. It flew down to attack her, but she slammed her door shut, and the creature took to scratching around outside her home. Neighborhood dogs came to the rescue to chase the big bird away. However, the next morning, all of the poor dogs were found dead.

The Lechuza isn't a thing of the past, either, and if anything appears to be becoming more prominent as opposed to being forgotten. For instance, in 2014, a video surfaced of people in rural Mexico burning a large owl alive because they were certain that it was actually a Lechuza…

La Llorona & Owls

*I*n New Mexico, the animal most associated with witches was the owl. Many a folktale was told where someone shot a suspicious-looking owl in the night, only to find an old woman suspected of being a witch dead the next morning. Or, if not deceased, at least injured in the same spot where the owl was shot. A few tales also associated La Llorona with owls, primarily due to her being conglomerated with witchcraft in many instances.

A tale from Mora, New Mexico, submitted by Margarita Olivas to authors Edward Garcia Kraul and Judith Beatty for their comprehensive work *The Weeping Woman: Encounters with La Llorona*, exemplified this best. Olivas told the authors, "My father used to tell me that La Llorona dressed like a witch."[1] She then went on to tell how they owned a meeting house in Mora, which owls ominously congregated about. Olivas recollected:

> Owls used to gather on the roof, sometimes ten at a time. My dad used to say they were witches. When they came down from the roof, they turned into women dressed in black. You couldn't see their faces. The leader was dressed in white and she was said to be *La Llorona*.[2]

Like other New Mexico witches, these owl-brujas were expelled with a simple religious exclamation of "*Jesus, Maria y Jose!*" Another account linking La Llorona to owls came from 1930s Santa Fe. A state penitentiary guard identified only as Tafoya was driving down a lonely road late at night when an owl flew in front of his headlights. Tafoya thought that either he or his car became bewitched by the owl, as the car seemed to follow the owl all the way to Guadalupe Cemetery. Tafoya parked the car and watched the owl soar over the graveyard and then disappear behind one of the headstones. From behind it arose a wailing woman dressed in all black. She walked through Tafoya's headlights, motioning behind her urgently as though she wished for him to do something. Free of the owl's bewitchment, he put the car in reverse and sped away. When he returned to the cemetery in daylight to look at the tombstone, he discovered it was for a deceased infant.

Section Notes

---

[1] Kraul and Beatty, *The Weeping Woman*, p.17.
[2] Ibid.

EL SILBÓN
THE WHISTLER

Although El Llorón should probably serve as La Llorona's true male counterpart, he is not terribly well-known when compared to El Silbón. The legend of El Silbón stemmed from Colombia and Venezuela, especially in the tropical grasslands collectively known as Los Llanos. Just as La Llorona is the crying woman, El Silbón is the whistling man, as his name literally means The Whistler.

El Silbón was usually depicted as a tall, lanky ghoul carrying a knapsack in which he carried human remains. Sometimes the specter was gigantic, standing twenty feet tall amidst the trees. Other times, his creeping shadow was said to stretch out to get his victims and he would eventually emerge from the shadow as he whistled. Sometimes he was zombie-like, with chunks of tattered flesh hanging from his emaciated frame. His signature attire comprised a straw hat and the bone-filled knapsack, said to creak as he walked. If a person was wandering alone at night and heard a whistling far, far away, they had better watch out, for that meant El Silbón was close at hand. However, if the whistling was close by, oddly enough, that meant the person was safe.

Like La Llorona sometimes did, El Silbón targeted unfaithful husbands and drunks. In the case of drunks, it was said that he would cut a hole in the drunk man's stomach, suck out all the

https://factschology.com/mmm-podcast-articles/el-silbon-whistling-man

El Silbón illustration c.1967.

alcohol, and then remove the man's bones to place in his knapsack. Worse yet, afterward, the man's soul was unable to cross over to the other side. Like El Silbón, they were cursed to wander Los Llanos for eternity until they could find El Silbón and reclaim their remains from his knapsack.

Whereas La Llorona served as a cautionary tale for bad parenting, El Silbón presented the case of an evil child. His origin story was that of a spoiled brat son whose parents catered to his every whim. The family, comprising of the mother, father, and grandfather, all lived together in Los Llanos in the 18th century. His fateful transition occurred one night when he demanded venison for dinner and sent his father out to hunt a deer. When his father failed to return home, the son became impatient. The mother suggested he go out and look for him in the woods, so the boy donned a knapsack and off he went, whistling as he walked. Eventually, the boy found his father sans the prized meat. The enraged teen took out his hunting knife and stabbed his father in spite of his apologies for not bagging a deer. He then proceeded to cut out his father's heart and liver and tossed his remains in the knapsack to carry them home. The boy took them to his mother to cook and serve for dinner, claiming that they were the deer meat and that his father would be back soon. However, the mother noticed the organs were unusually tough for those of a deer, so she went to investigate and found her husband's bones and mutilated remains in her son's knapsack.

She ran to tell the grandfather of his grandson's horrid crime, and the grandfather had the boy captured and tied to a post. The mother put a curse on her son and the grandfather proceeded to whip his back. Then, he cleaned the open wounds with the most painful remedies he could, including lemon juice, chili peppers, and alcohol. The grandfather untied his grandson and placed upon his back the knapsack containing the remains of his murdered father. The grandfather put his own curse on the grandson that he carry his father's remains for all eternity. Lastly, he set two hunting dogs loose to chase the boy, who ran away to become El Silbón.

Engraving by Jose Guadalupe Posada (1852-1913).

As to be expected, there are many versions of the tale, and in one the hunting dogs tore the boy apart on the spot rather than chasing him into the jungle. In yet another, the dog was more of a supernatural hellhound bound to chase him for eternity.

Due to the way that he died, the sound of barking dogs were able to repel El Silbón, as could the cracking of a whip. Chili peppers could also be used to ward him off. Interestingly, it was said that El Silbón would sit outside of a family home whistling as he counted the bones on the porch. If everyone heard the whistle, everyone was safe. If only one person heard the whistle, then they were marked for death.

Like other specters in this book, sometimes El Silbón had a tenuous connection to water in the form of rain. Specifically, it was said that El Silbón was practically harmless during the drought season in Venezuela. Furthermore, if one saw El Silbón sitting in the trees, it was a sure sign the drought would continue. But, when the rains returned, so would El Silbón.

THE BABY MONSTER

CHILD OF LA LLORONA?

On a warm spring night in Santa Fe in 1945, two men were walking down Romero Street on their way home from the pool hall close to midnight. As they approached the railroad tracks, a ball of fire suddenly rolled in their direction. Almost immediately, the orb of fire turned into "a bundle wrapped in a patchwork quilt."[1] The bundle came to a stop about 20 feet away, and so they trepidly approached it. Soon, they could hear the sound of a baby crying. They unwrapped the quilt to find a frightening apparition. Within was what appeared to be a six-month-old baby, only it had fangs and a gruesome face. In an account from one of the men's relatives, it was written that "It opened its mouth as if to cry, but instead, it smiled at them and said, '*Mira, Daddy, tengo dientes*—Look, Daddy, I have teeth.'"[2]

The two men ran home in terror, and soon after, one of the men's hair turned snow white. When they told their family the tale, they swore it was the child of La Llorona. A similar Santa Fe-based tale, taking place on an unknown date, concerned a man only identified as Mr. Garcia, who went out drinking on Good Friday despite his wife's warnings that he would be cursed for it. As he stumbled home later that night, he saw an apparition of a woman in white. He ran all the way home, and when he arrived, he found a mysterious baby wrapped in a white blanket in his driveway. Unfolding it, he found not a baby, but a miniature La Llorona with dark, black eyes and a bony hand pointing at him. He dropped the demonic baby, ran inside, and never took another drink for the rest of his life.

Though both stories chose to throw in La Llorona, in fact, they were variations of a common Spanish folktale where a mysterious baby found along the roadside sprouted fangs and turned into a monster. In Stanley Robe's compilation, *Hispanic Legends from New Mexico*, the author summarized the basic legend thusly,

> The narrative of the apparently abandoned baby who develops long fangs and acquires the ability to speak is well known to New Mexican informants. All texts begin with the finding of what appears to be a hopeless infant who suddenly takes on the features of a malevolent spirit. This startling change and the fright that overcomes the finder are consistent features of the story.[3]

Other popular variations of the legend usually entailed a young man riding his horse late one night. Usually, he would be going to or from either a dance or the home of his girlfriend when he would hear the cry of a baby. After rescuing the child, it would then begin exhibiting fearsome characteristics. One unique alteration of the "baby monster" story chose to make it the origin of La Llorona herself. It was collected from Mora and was included in *Hispanic Legends from New Mexico*:

> One time there were four men coming home from a dance in Buena Vista, a little village about 13 miles from Mora. As they approached a bridge, they heard someone crying. It sounded like a small child and they stopped to investigate. One of the men saw a little girl about two years old running towards him and she was crying. He got off his horse and picked her up. She was very pretty and she was dressed in white. He decided to keep her until he could find out who she belonged to.
>
> When he took his leave from the other four men, he started toward his home and was admiring the beauty of

this child. He said, "My, you are a pretty little girl! I wish that you were mine."

She replied, "Yes, and I also have teeth." This astonished the man and he immediately dropped her and got off his horse. He picked up a stone to throw at her and she was still muttering, "Yes, and I also have teeth." He threw the stone and she disappeared. Sometime later when these men were coming through this bridge again, they still heard the wailing of a little girl. Today they call her "La Llorona."

Another account appearing in the same book and coming from Las Vegas utilized another variation of the myth. Although La Llorona was not mentioned, the fact that the baby was linked to a dead wife and a drainage ditch made it tangential:

A man was going to a dance two days after he had buried his wife, who had died. On his way to the dance he heard a baby cry. He got off his horse and found an infant in a ditch. He took off his coat and wrapped the baby and went on his way. The baby would laugh and talk with him. He noticed smoke coming out of his coat. He opened the coat and the baby disappeared.

Were these baby monsters the lost children of La Llorona up to their own hauntings or just the result of old-timers mixing popular myths together? Most likely, it was a case of the latter and showed how easily common folktales could cross-pollinate.

Chapter Notes

[1] Kraul and Beatty, *The Weeping Woman*, p.3.
[2] Ibid.
[3] Robe, *Hispanic Legends from New Mexico*, p.158.

From the *Chicago Tribune* of October 21, 1906.

GHOST RIDER
OF THE MIMBRES

BLACK RANGE BEAUTY

In place of La Llorona, a benevolent female ghost once haunted the arid Mimbres of southwestern New Mexico. It was John L. Sinclair who resurrected the long-dormant ghost in his book *Cowboy Riding Country*, notably comparing her to La Llorona and claiming that "Of all the ghosts that have ever haunted New Mexico, there was none like the Ghost Girl of the Mimbres."[1] Other sources described her as a "graceful horsewoman, meticulously garbed and with physical features as beautiful as ever seen on any female" of about twenty years of age.[2] Because women were a rarity in the Back Range country apart from the wives and daughters of local ranchers, to see such a beautiful woman riding alone in the middle of the wilderness was shocking for those who saw her.

The story was first reported in the *Chicago Tribune* on October 21, 1906, chronicling a flap of ghost sightings that occurred earlier that summer in a faraway New Mexico. A cowboy named Pete Bianca was the first to record the ghost when he saw it at the Crossing of the Mimbres in May of 1906. "The mystery is a girl, young, handsome, fearless, an expert rider, who, mounted on a big bay horse, rides by night and by day, appears at points dozens of miles apart, and who cannot be located, and of whom no trace except when she appears suddenly before some surprised cow puncher can be found," the article began. It continued,

According to the descriptions given by those who have seen her, the girl is tall, slender, browned by the sun and desert winds laden with alkali. She is the most beautiful woman ever seen in a land where all of the women are handsome, making up in beauty what they lack in numbers. She is the most graceful rider in all that part of the country, where all the women are graceful riders.

She is tall, dark, yet not of the Spanish type, with brown hair and perfect features. Her horse is as perfect physically as she, for the best range horses in the territory cannot catch her when she flees.

The cow punchers speak of her in whispers of awe as "the ghost woman." And, fearing nothing, they vow that even yet they will catch her and discover whether she is flesh and blood or spirit. The miners along the Black Range and up in the Burros vow they will trap her yet when she crosses the passes of the mountains.

Pete Bianca glimpsed her along the Santa Fe Trail on his way to interview for a job at the Desdemona Mine not too far from Cook's Peak. He was riding through the adobe ruins of Mowrey, by then a ghost town, when he spotted the beautiful rider. "He was riding along carelessly, when suddenly he saw the girl, mounted on the horse, centering along down the trail, which at that point runs through a little grove of cottonwoods. She was wearing a wide felt hat, a khaki colored riding suit, and patent leather boots, while on her heels silver spurs clinked."

Panorama of Fort Bayard.

From a distance, Pete watched as the woman dismounted her horse to get a drink from a small stream. When she headed off in the direction of his friend Dan Taylor's ranch, he decided to follow assuming she might be his wife. Eventually he lost sight of the woman, and when he arrived at Taylor's ranch, his friend answered that he had no wife nor any female companions at the ranch. "[Taylor] told Pete he was crazy for the lack of sense, that there was no woman nearer than Cooks. He even declared no woman had passed in that direction," the paper said.

To prove it to Taylor, Pete made him ride out to see the woman's tracks for himself, which disappeared into a gully not far from the ranch house. A week later, the ghostly beauty was seen again in the vicinity of Santa Rita, a mining town, by Ed Tuttle. Either considering it too forward to speak, or perhaps he was simply too nervous, it was all Tuttle could do to tip his sombrero to her as his horse outpaced hers on the way into town. When Tuttle inquired amongst friends as to the beautiful woman's identity, they all just laughed and said it must have been the same specter glimpsed by Pete Bianca. Undeterred, Tuttle went to every hotel and boarding house in the area to inquire about the girl, but to no avail. When someone speculated she might be a visitor from Silver City, Tuttle traveled there to look for her. Again, there was no trace or record of any such woman.

Tuttle's next idea was that perhaps she was the daughter of an old soldier at Fort Bayard. This was where Tuttle finally caught a lead, though it wasn't what he was expecting. A soldier from Fort Bayard had indeed seen the girl before in the hills near Georgetown. "I passed her on the road, and, thinking she might be one of the officers' ladies, I spoke and raised my hat," the officer told Tuttle. He continued, "She did not speak. I rode beside her a few minutes and then she suddenly wheeled her horse and galloped the other way."

When Tuttle asked what happened, the soldier responded, "Well, I haven't told anyone, because they'd think I was crazy. But that girl disappeared right in the middle of the road while I was watching her. I've been puzzled over it ever since."

Having heard that the woman vanished into thin air, then clearly she must be a ghost. The tale spread like wildfire, and soon every cowpuncher in the region was determined to find the girl and prove that she was a flesh and blood woman rather than a specter. One night in July, cowpuncher Bert Cooper caught a glimpse of her in the moonlight. It was a hair past ten outside of Silver City, where Cooper had been frequenting the saloons. When he gave chase to the beautiful apparition, her ghostly horse easily outpaced his own:

> The girl appeared not to notice the clatter of his cow horse's hoofs, but when he was within 200 yards of her she turned her horse swiftly and rode on. Cooper spurred and lashed his horse, one of the best in the country, and, although he extended it to the utmost and the girl's horse did not seem to be trying, it gained steadily, and finally she disappeared, whither Bert does not know.

Soon after, a cowboy called Navajo Andrews not only glimpsed her, but briefly interacted with her. He was south of Deming in the Florida Mountains when he saw the girl riding in daylight. He called out to her, and she acknowledged his greeting with a wave and then rode away. A cowpuncher named Fletch Burke reported her next, claiming she rode up beside him on a late-night roundup. When he spoke to her, she didn't respond and rode away. Like the others, he was unable to catch up with her.

The Florida Mountains in Deming.

The Ghost of the Mimbres made her exit into one of the most notable locales of the region, that being the City of Rocks, a natural formation of rock pillars. The witnesses comprised cowboys from the Flying Y Ranch north of Deming, including Sam Teener, Manuelo Yeros, and Mont Steen. It was early September, and the three men first spotted her sitting atop her horse and gazing at the City of Rocks in the distance.

> The trio of cowpunchers stopped and gazed in surprise. The girl had removed her hat and her beautiful brown hair was blowing free about her perfect face.
>
> The three men held a consultation and decided that they would unravel the mystery, even if they were forced to rope the girl and make her tell who she was, what she was, and why she was there.
>
> This is the way Sam Teener tells it:
>
> "We rode up to within fifty yards of her before she seemed to notice us. I called out, 'Hello' and she glanced up. I started to ride up to her. She never made a move. I called, 'Good-morning. Miss!' and she smiled and touched her horse with her spurs. If I had moved quick then, I might have reached her, but before I got over

wondering at her beauty her horse was sure moving. I started after her and called out to Monty to head her off. I see in a minute that Manuelo is no good, because he's hunting his crucifix and crossing himself.

City of Rocks as depicted on vintage postcard.

"That girl sure had some horse. He simply galloped away from us and I was riding breeze, and we were going some ourselves. She rode straight at the City of Rocks, with me an eighth of a mile behind. I thought she would swing around them rocks and skirt the city to the west, but she rode as if she was going straight in. She swerved a bit just as she reached the first bowlders and I lost sight of her for a second. There is no bowlder for 100 yards between the bowlder she disappeared behind and the beginning of the city proper—but that girl never came out from behind the first big bowlder. We scattered and surrounded the city, watching for her, and I hunted for tracks. I could trace her plainly enough to the big bowlder and for perhaps twenty yards on the other side of it—then I lost the track entirely.

"I don't know what to make of it. How she got away I don't know. She ain't a ghost, although Manuelo swears she is. I know she isn't, because while I was riding towards her and she was sitting there watching the city,

I saw her pull a hairpin out of her hair and squint up her face while she held it in her mouth until she got ready to pin down a stray bit of hair.

"Ghosts don't use hairpins, no matter what Manuelo says—and them wasn't ghost hairpins, because I found one of them. I'd like to have the chance to return it."

After this, it's debatable if the beautiful mirage was ever seen again. According to Ruth Brown, director of the Deming Luna Mimbres Museum in 1994, one could still see the Ghost Girl of the Mimbres "every now and then on the Silver City Highway."[3] Other than that fleeting mention from 1994, not much else is said of the Ghost Girl of the Mimbres. If her spectral form still rides the Black Range, the witnesses are keeping their sightings to themselves.

Chapter Notes

---

[1] Sinclair, *Cowboy Riding Country*, 143.
[2] Robe, *Hispanic Legends from New Mexico*, p.144.
[3] Speer, "Local ghost stories, sites delight Demingites," *The Deming Headlight* (October 31, 1994).

NUECES RIVER'S WAILING WOMAN

THE TRAGEDY OF CHIPITA RODRÍGUEZ

A Texas legend tangent to La Llorona is that of Chipita Rodríguez. For many years, Chipita was notorious as the first woman to be legally hanged in Texas, and on Friday the 13th no less. She ran a small boarding house along the Nueces River in 1863 and was executed for brutally murdering a man—a crime she was likely innocent of. As it was, Chipita was an elderly woman who barely weighed 100 pounds when she was accused of the crime.

Most sources say that Chipita was born in Mexico around New Year's Eve of 1799 and came to Texas with her father, who was part of the Mexican army during Santa Anna's march to San Antonio in 1836. However, her father, Pedro Rodríguez, deserted the army to take his wife and child to the Nueces River near an Irish settlement called San Patricio. As Chipita grew to womanhood, legend holds that, like La Llorona, she married and had a baby. But unfortunately, her husband left her and took the baby with him. Now a spinster, Chipita ran a small boarding house, really more of a *jacal* (hut) along the Nueces River. During the Civil War in August of 1863, a horse trader named John Savage was passing through San Patricio on his way to Corpus Christi. At a local saloon, he bragged of a big sale he had recently made to the Confederate Army before going on to Chipita's jacal, where he stayed the night.

Undated newspaper photo of the area where Chipita was hanged.

A few days later, Savage's corpse was found in a burlap bag floating down the river. His head had been split open by an ax. Bags containing $600 worth of gold coins belonging to Savage were found nearby, and the blame was placed on Chipita. She was arrested by Sheriff William B. Means and she repeatedly cried out, "No soy culpable." ("I am not guilty.") Also arrested was Chipita's slow-witted servant boy, Juan Silvera. Rumors circulated that not only was Silvera her illegitimate son, but that perhaps he had killed Savage and Chipita was protecting him.

As to why Chipita and Silvera were suspected, it was said that an ax was found covered in blood at Chipita's jacal. That she and Silvera often used that same ax to behead chickens wasn't a strong enough argument to get Chipita acquitted. Actually, Chipita didn't even receive representation at her trial, and nor could she speak English to the predominantly Irish townsfolk. The jury at Chipita's trial pleaded mercy for the old woman due to her age, but the judge would not have it.[1] While Silvera was sentenced to serve five years in prison, Chipita would be executed on November 13, 1863. On that day, she was taken to a grove of trees along the river and hanged from the tallest oak they could find.

Ominously, one recounting stated that "a heavy, billowing grey mass rolled in from the Gulf and blotted out the sun."[2] Some even said that the poor old woman's legs were shackled as she marched to her doom.[3] Nor was it a swift death. She was stood on the back of an old ox cart, and when it pulled out from beneath her, it didn't snap her neck. Instead, she swung back and forth as she slowly strangled to death. Some accounts went that the hangman, John Gilpin, wrapped a bandana around her face, while others said no face coverings were used and onlookers watched in horror as Chiptia's face contorted as she strangled. (Afterward, the villagers were so disgusted that they refused to help the hangman dig the grave.) Chipita was placed in a cypress coffin and buried under the hanging tree.

Artist's rendition of Chipita.

One man claimed he heard a ghostly wail come from the coffin before it was buried. Another rendition had the witness hearing a thump and a groan as though she was being buried alive. Odder yet, the tree was struck by lightning soon after the hanging and died. Some say nothing will grow near the spot where she was hanged, either. One of the Irish onlookers supposedly stated the following as they left the execution: "Tis a black day for San Patricio. Tis a curse we have brought upon our town."[4] Perhaps they were right, for eventually San Patricio became a ghost town and today its claim to fame is Chipita, regarded as a wrongly accused fatality of frontier justice.

Like La Llorona, Chipita wandered and wailed along the local rivers for many years, sometimes seen with the noose still around her neck. In addition to the river, supposedly Chipita's ghost haunted Silvera, her servant boy, after he was released from prison. She was also seen in the boarding house of Miss Lida Dougherty in the 1930s. Miss Dougherty was said to remark of the execution, "Could a more unholy or unnatural thing have happened in an Irish village?"

Still, most saw her spectral shadow gliding near the site of her old jacal, forever calling out, "No soy culpable." Chipita's cries were heard, albeit much too late. She was officially pardoned in 1985, and a historical marker was placed near the site of her hanging in 2010.[5] Interestingly, since her pardon, sightings waned until the wailing woman was seen no more.

"Many persons have claimed they saw Chipita walking slowly along the riverbank, the frayed noose dangling from her neck," said *The Baytown Sun* of June 13, 1960.

Chapter Notes

[1] The judge was Benjamin F. Neal, later the first mayor of Corpus Christi.
[2] McDaneil, "The Day They Hanged Chipita," *Kerrville Mountain Sun* (December 12, 1962), p.5.
[3] Because she had no dress for her hanging, one villager gave her an old wedding dress to wear, technically making her a Woman in White.
[4] McDaneil, "The Day They Hanged Chipita," *Kerrville Mountain Sun* (December 12, 1962), p.5.
[5] About 25 years after her hanging, a 71-year-old man who was near death confessed that he had killed Savage all those years ago.

VOLCANO MONSTER
OF LA MALINCHE
MALINTZIN'S REPTILIAN MENACE

In the Mexican states of Tlaxcala and Puebla exists the dormant volcano known by the varying names of La Malinche, Matlalcueye, and Malintzin. Inactive for the last three millennia, La Malinche is the sixth-highest peak in all of Mexico and the tallest in Tlaxcala with a maximum altitude of 4,461 meters above sea level. The volcano is also home to a monster. The landscape is a perfect haunt for a mythical creature, too. The craggy volcanic summit is surrounded not only by a forest of pines, but some barren, windswept plains nearer the volcano itself.

The description of the creature was vague other than the fact that it was reptilian in nature. So the story went, during the rainy season, it would slither down from its volcano lair to kidnap children from the village below. It would then drag its terrified victims back to its mountain abode, trudging through the sleet and frost too difficult for mere mortals to traverse. Then, somewhere amidst the craggy, volcanic rock, the reptilian monster would devour the children.

While it may sound like your basic boogeyman, the creature is actually related to La Llorona through its namesake, La Malinche. One of La Malinche's greatest achievements was winning over the Tlaxcala Kingdom in favor of Cortés against the Aztecs. As covered earlier, according to myth, La Malinche bore Cortés a child and may have been the original La Llorona. As an alternative to this myth, and rather than killing her infant son, some Tlaxcalans believed that La Malinche ascended the dormant volcano for solace after being betrayed by Cortés and never returned.[1] As such, some visitors believe they can feel the sad, lonely spirit of La Malinche on the mountain.

What's In a Name? Having noted the parallel between La Malinche and La Llorona, coincidentally or not, the alternate name for the mountain has yet another tie to La Llorona. The name given to the volcano by the Tlaxcaltecs was Matlalcueitl, which translates to "Lady of the Blue Skirt." This was itself a nod to their version of the goddess Chalchiuhtlicu. Specifically, she was the Aztec goddess of rivers, streams, and childbirth. Water and children, as we know, are La Llorona's two main calling cards.

With La Malinche as one of the archetypes of La Llorona, the fact that the volcano that bears her name is associated with a monster that preys upon children is undeniably interesting. The Tlaxcala region was also notorious for an epidemic of infant deaths throughout the 1950s and the early 1960s. As it stands, though it had no physical resemblance to the vampire women of Tlaxcala, the Malinche volcano monster did have the same modus operandi, that being that it preyed upon children during the rainy months. Modern accounts of the monster are vague aside from those given by David Bowles and Robert Bitto. In his *Mexican Bestiary*, Bowles described the monster specifically as being in "the shape of a man but [with] the head of a snake."[2] In addition to its reptile form, on Mexico Unexplained, Bitto noted that the monster was also sometimes depicted as a hairy giant, like Bigfoot. Like the monster's varying description, its origins were equally vague but, according to Bitto,

> The creature was supposedly created by a group of indigenous sorcerers who belonged to the Popoloca tribe who had grown weary of Spanish abuses and decided to manifest a monster to terrorize colonial settlements.[3]

Both Bowles and Bitto related what was either a folktale, or possibly a real event from the Puebla's past concerning the monster. What follows will be a combination of both. The basic account began with a well-to-do merchant named Pedro de Carvajal living in Puebla during the early colonial period. Carvajal had two children, a daughter, Teodora, and a son, Fernando. Sadly, Don Pedro's wife died while giving birth to Fernando. Teodora, according to the more detailed account, was nine years old when this occurred. Initially, servants and assorted nannies helped raise the two children, but eventually Teodora took on the role of mother to her little brother. When Fernando was six and Teodora was by now fifteen, the beautiful young woman was courted by a soldier named Juan Luis Caballero. Though some said Don Pedro denied Caballero's advances because he considered a soldier to be beneath his daughter, perhaps he simply didn't want to become a single father to young Fernando. Not long after, the monster of La Malinche began its depredations. For several weeks during the rainy season, it came down from the mountain to terrorize Puebla at night, abducting children to take to its mountain lair where it devoured them slowly.

In broad daylight, the monster came for little Fernando and, according to Bitto, snatched the boy away while he was playing in front of the Carvajal home. In Bowles' version, the monster took Fernando to the town square of Puebla where it devoured him in front of horrified onlookers. The grief-stricken Don Pedro offered a substantial reward—some say nearly all that he had—for the killing of the monster. He even had a special hoop mounted above his front door so that the monster's head could be placed there once it was severed from its body. No one was bold enough to brave the monster's mountain lair but the jilted soldier, Caballero. Killing the monster would not only serve as an act of love on behalf of the grieving Teodora, but it would also no doubt win her hand in the eyes of her father.

Puebla.   Los Volcanes.

Though some claim that it was a heartbroken Malinche who ascended the dormant volcano in Tlaxcala, earlier legends told of another heartbroken girl who did so. She was Matlalcueye, a maiden engaged to Cuatlapanga, a warrior who had left to go off to war. When Cuatlapanga was gone for too long, Matlalcueye died of sorrow. When Cuatlapanga returned and learned that his betrothed was dead, he went to her grave and wept until he died himself. The combined power of his love and grief is what created Cuatlapanga, a smaller mountain flanking Malinche. Matlalcueye then turned into the even larger volcano now called Malinche.

And so, Caballero announced that with the help of God and the Virgin, he would behead the beast. However, the knight didn't even have to track the dragon to its lair. Instead, he came across it on another one of its raids in the Puebla plaza. Though his horse reared up, frightened of the monster, Caballero managed to strike a blow against the creature with his lance. The monster ran away with Caballero in pursuit. Finally cornering the wounded fiend, he beheaded it with a single blow from his sword. Caballero arrived at Don Pedro's home soon after with the monster's head impaled on his lance. The head was placed in the hoop above the door, and Caballero was allowed to court Teodora as hoped. And, not only did he eventually marry Teodora, but he was also given an unspecified title from the government thanks to his heroism.[4]

Frog Goddesses of the Pacific Northwest

Another tie to the legend of La Malinche volcano monster is the fact that the Aztecs had several gods that were reptilian in nature. Cihuacoatl's name translated to Snake Woman, for instance. Interestingly, the Aztec goddess Cihuacoatl was occasionally depicted as a toad woman, which is relevant to this chapter due to a tangential legend to Cihuacoatl in the Pacific Northwest. In his article "La Llorona and Related Themes," author Bacil F. Kirtley more or less argued that the North Pacific version of La Llorona/Cihuacoatl, called Dzelarkhons, may have been inspired by Central American legends. Notably, Dzelarkhons was also known as the "Weeping Woman" but was associated with frogs. Carvings depicted her as a weeping woman, holding her dead child, and whose teardrops turn into tiny frogs. More interesting than that, though, is the fact that this weeping frog woman was also associated with volcanoes, much like the reptilian menace of La Malinche.

Dzelarkhons wasn't the only weeping frog woman known to the indigenous tribes of North America. Another came from the Algonkian tribe in central Maine, which spoke of two frog demons known as Pskégdemus and Maski'kcwsu. The former cried out in longing for either a man or a child to call her own, and anyone who pitied her was likely to disappear forever. The latter was often called the Toad Woman, who despite the unattractive name was thought of as a seducer of men and children. Kirtley believed that these Toad Women could have been Mexican legends that migrated north thanks to the Spaniards as they traveled into North America.

However, perhaps a more plausible explanation might simply be that these indigenous peoples encountered similar supernatural creatures, thus explaining the similarities. (The serpentine qualities of Lilith, one of the premiere progenitors of La Llorona, were covered in the very first chapter as only one instance.) Ultimately, considering how many different La Lloronas are out there haunting the world, there has to be something to them more than legend.

Puebla postcard, c.1940s, with the volcano in the background.

While the story had all the trappings of a medieval tale of knights slaying dragons, there were and still are people who believe the story to be true. Bowles related that the house of Carvajal, where the monstrous head was displayed, is still located in Puebla's historical district. According to Bowles, the building was roughly known as *the house of he who slew the animal* and later became the Hotel Italia, and after that, the main office of the Mexican Press Organization, which publishes the *Pueblan Sun*. According to Bowles, "Above the entrance to the building, visitors can behold, carved into stone, an image of the soldier, fighting against the monster."[5]

Chapter Notes

[1] It's important to note that I have never come across stories that imply Malinche fled to the mountain after killing her children, nor that she became the monster (though I'm surprised that speculation has never been put forth). In fact, some stories portrayed Malinche's ghost as a spiritual protector and a benevolent figure as opposed to a wraith. Supposedly, offerings were even made to La Malinche there and rituals performed.

[2] Bowles, *Mexican Bestiary*, p.118.

[3] Bitto, "Seven Brief Legends from Puebla," Mexico Unexplained. https://mexicounexplained.com/seven-brief-legends-from-puebla/

[4] Bitto's variation of the tale had the suitor of low birth turn down the reward money simply for a chance at courting Teodora.

[5] Bowles, *Mexican Bestiary*, p.118.

APPENDIX I
Origin Stories

This origin story for La Llorona was printed in newspapers in the year 1888, and this particular rendition came from the Wichita Eagle *out of Kansas on May 12, 1888:*

A LEGEND OF MEXICO

It was 3 o'clock in the morning. The bells of the cathedral and the palace, far away, struck the hour, as we traversed a lonely, silent street toward the suburbs of Mexico. We had been keeping vigil with a wounded man, a compatriot of mine, and had overstayed our watch, for he was frantic with delirium, and we feared to transfer him to the care of the inexperienced and rather careless persons who should succeed us.

We walked on briskly, for it was long hours past the time when coaches and tramcars had ceased plying. We were in San Cosme, and in front of the great, massive structure which the wife of ex-Marshal Bazaine has claimed from the government as an imperial gift to her traitorous husband. The facade of this edifice curves in in such fashion as to form an offset or alcove on the street, and before we reached it, I fancied I saw a woman's figure stealing along in its denser shadow, and I felt a thrill of compassion for her, as one of the poor children of the night. She was not to be seen when we came near the spot, but a moment later a piercing cry rang out near us—a long drawn wail of suffering and horror.

I grasped the arm of my comrade. "Some woman is in distress— we must go to her rescue. We are both armed, thank heaven!"

But he threw his arm about me, and forced me forward at a quick pace that was almost a run; and so unexpected was the move that I had been pushed along some rods ere I could offer resistance.

"Come on! come on!" he whispered hoarsely, as I shook myself free from his clasp. "We must hasten; we must go on quickly!"

"I would not have believed you could desert a fellow creature in trouble!" I cried in indignation, "and beyond all, a woman. It is not like you, Federico." For I had seen his courage tried by venomous serpents in tierra caliente, and in encounters with highwaymen in the Sierras, and I had heard of his coolness and daring in a combat with Apaches in northern Chihuahua.

"Hush! hush!" he answered, panting. "You know not of what you speak. We abandon no mortal woman—the voice you hear is the cry of La Llorona. Look yonder at the sereno!"

We were near one of the points where a watchman stands all night in the middle of a thoroughfare, and, following my companion's gesture, I saw the officer, fallen upon his knees in the circle of light cast by his lantern; the great hood of his cape was pulled over his head, and every line of his figure betokened abject fear and horror. There was something uncanny in the sight, for the policemen of Mexico are not impressionable material. And through the silent, empty street those dreadful cries were still ringing wildly, surely sufficient motive for such a display of terror. The sound seemed to float away, and down a by street toward the equestrian statue of Charles IV, growing fainter and fainter in the distance.

"Let us go," said my companion. "Yes, I am materialista, and I sneer at spiritualism and ghosts and phantoms; but, nevertheless, I think there is not a man or woman in Mexico who would not tremble at the voice of Luisa La Llorona."

***

In the year of our Lord 1584, Luisa Haro was called the most beautiful girl in Mexico, and the most modest. Her father had brought her from Spain when she was 10 years old, and, dying four years later, had left her utterly without kindred, so far as was known to herself or her neighbors. She was a clever needle woman, and a maker of artificial flowers, and her skill found ready employment for churchly uses, notwithstanding the enormous quantity of such work done in the convents. She had her little home nest in a lonely callejuela, or by street, almost like an alley, in the shadow of the cloister walls of one of the guilds that chiefly employed her, and here she lived, forlornly enough, indeed, as is the fate of a woman who dwells quite alone; but her days were virtuous and tranquil. Naught mattered it to her that the gallants came stealing at nightfall into that rincon apartado—that out of the way corner, and tenanted the midnight darkness of its dusty, narrow passage. Her shutters were closed and barred ere the darkness gathered, and none of the delicate, scented fingers that tapped on those clumsy defenses ever sounded the "Open, Sesame!" to the girl they sheltered. Luisa was the despair of all the gay, dissolute blades of the vice regal court of

New Spain. Her neighbors in the lonely by street were wont to point her out with a strange admixture of feelings, uncertain whether to respect and recommend her severe rectitude, or to disparage her, as one who is denied the natural passions and pleasant frailties of humanity.

But a change came about when the girl was something over 20 years old. It began to be whispered by the gossips of the neighborhood that the shutters of Luisa's window now creaked slightly open, and that her voice was heard at the crevice in converse with one who came not tentatively and doubting, but with the confident, assured step of a man who knows the welcome that awaits him. And soon it was told about, originated in one of the vague, indefinite ways in which such things do transpire, that this complacent wooer was Nuno, Marquis of Montes-Claros. So it was that Luisa assumed a new importance in the eyes of those about her, as will ever happen, under like conditions.

One night—a night when the dashing rain scourged the black walls of the cloister, to the mournful accompaniment of the moaning owls in the belfry—one of the parish goodmen was hastening home belated through the narrow callejuela where dwelt Luisa, when he saw in the space before him something that made him pause and tremble, for he was of the timid bourgeois class that carried no staunch Toledo blade nor slender deadly rapier swung from the belt.

The night was dark, almost to palpability. No ray of light fell into the callejuela, save the dim ray from the little lantern, swinging before the rude image of some saint in a niche near the tablet on the wall, at the entrance of the by street where it opened with a blunt angle into a wider thoroughfare. That ray, falling through the weather stained pane of the lantern, was dim and fitful, and almost seemed to make the darkness denser, and more concrete than the shapes that the honest wayfarer fancied he saw flitting along the wall. Now these might be some of the gallants that were always wrangling hereabouts for the sweet sake of Luisa, albeit there had been a notable failing off in their attendance, since it was rumored she had finally hearkened to the voice of one of their number. Or—and the hair of the honest fellow bristled at the idea, for all the darkness—it might even be Don Nuno himself, and his worship, by all accounts, would not hesitate to spit like a curlew from the marshes one whom he might meet poaching on his preserves. So, fearing to be mistaken for a gallant, the honest citizen shrunk into himself, and flattened his portliness against the convent wall as best might be. And the vague shapes passed him by in silence unperceiving.

He repented him of his timidity the next morning and reviled himself for a fool, a coward, when the neighborhood thrilled to the flight of Luisa Haro. Her door stood ajar, and the poor belongings of her stood undisturbed in order. All the evidence pointed to the fact that her flight was voluntary and deliberate, and the popular voice was unanimous in declaring that her comrade must be Nuno, Marquis of Montes-Claros. It was this pair, no doubt, whom the worthy goodman had seen stealing away through the darkness, and his repentance was keen that he had not followed them, to possess himself of that knowledge of their movements and destination that would have made him important among his fellows.

From that day her old time neighbors knew naught of Luisa Haro, save that someone, whose affairs had taken him to the suburbs of San Cosme, brought back the story that he had seen her there, blooming and with sumptuous accessories, in the balcony of a splendid mansion that was known to belong to Montes-Claros.

***

Six years after the flight of Luisa from her homely abode in the narrow callejuela she sat in the luxurious home where Montes-Claros had placed her, brooding mournfully over her situation. The moonlight streamed through the open window and illuminated her despondent figure. In face and form she was more beautiful than on the day she fled with Montes-Claros, but still was she not beautiful enough to keep the fickle fancy of the Spaniard. His attentions and his interest had gradually diminished, until the unhappy woman now had but too much reason to consider herself altogether deserted by him, for whom she had given up all that is most dear to women. She had lacked no material comfort, it is true, thus far, but this was little consolation to a woman whose thwarted affection was as strong and unaltered as when her passionate heart first poured out its ardent incense before her lover.

She had not seen Montes-Claros for a fortnight, and she was resolved to know the worst without further horror of suspense and anxiety. She rose and carried the infant in her arms to an alcove, behind whose silken curtains lay two older children sleeping. She laid the little one beside its brothers. She shrouded herself in a long, dark, clinging mantle, left the house, and took her way to the central streets of the city.

She knew the family mansion of Montes-Claros, and shortly found herself before it. The windows of the facade were ablaze with light, and the alarmed watcher saw that the rooms were full of a festive throng. Nuno was there in the midst of his guests with his proud, affected mother, and beside them a young girl, tall and handsome, in bridal raiment.

The heart of Luisa sank like lead within her. She plucked by the sleeve a bystander, gazing like herself through the window. "Do you know, friend, who is the young lady beside the Senor Marques?"

"Who should it be," laughed the man she questioned, "but his novia—the bride he wedded this morning at 10 of the clock in the Chapel of the Sagrario."

No word answered Luisa, but neither made she outcry, only presently fell back from the window, and pushed her way to the open street through the eager crowd of onlookers.

Slowly, mechanically, she held her way, never hastening, never pausing, till she reached the house in San Cosme, and let herself in at its great arched entrance, and into her own chamber. An antique coffer stood there, an ancient cedar chest with Mauresque decoration, brought over from Spain by the family of Montes-Claros. In it Nuno had been wont to deposit, while he yet frequented the dwelling, such odds and ends as, fancying, he might buy on the way out thither, or matters in his possession at the moment that he found cumbrous.

Still under the spell of that awful, deadly quiet, Luisa opened the old chest, and took from it a dagger, a curious jeweled weapon, that Nuno had tossed down long months since, and forgotten, though its memory had lived in the fevered brain of the woman.

Still lighted by the pallid, ghastly moonbeams, she went to the alcove where her little ones lay sleeping, and drew aside the curtains.

"Your father has forsaken us, my darling ones, and your mother would fain preserve you from the miseries that await you. To God I recommend your innocent spirits."

Then, one by one, slowly, surely, fatally, she thrust the dagger into the bosom of each tender little body.

Only when the blood welled darkly up, staining the white night raiment, did the wretched mother seem to realize her dreadful doing. She gazed a moment at the heart rending vision, and then ran forth into the streets, uttering those frightful wails that for 300 years have continued to echo in the streets of Mexico at varying hours and seasons—when the soul in penance can no longer endure its torture, so the devout say.

As the wailing woman ran that night her cries aroused the city, and she was captured and recognized, when the dagger she still clutched and her blood stained raiment told the tragic story and gave the clew to discovery of her victims. There was no penalty for man's inhumanity to woman in the Mexico of those days any more than in the present, and the poor, distracted instrument of crime paid all the temporal penalty in this case, while the actual murderer, in fact, rather gained popularity.

During her imprisonment and trial Luisa maintained a helpless, hopeless silence. She failed and faded day by day, and when at last arrived the hour of execution she was unable to walk up the steps of the scaffold, and, not from fright, but sheer weakness, she became senseless in the arms of her bearers. The execution proceeded, but the decree of the law was done on a corpse, for ere the halter touched her Luisa Haro was lifeless.

And however justice had miscarried in the hands of human authority, the retribution of heaven proved direct and active; for on that very May day, when the woman who had trusted him went to the doom of a felor, Nuno, Marquis of Montes-Claros, was buried, having died ere his honeymoon was over.

And now, centuries after it, it is told that whenever appears the Wailing Woman the following morning sees the flowers on the tomb of Montes-Claros withered, seared, and the earth upon it dank and noisome, as if it were drenched and soaked with blood.—Y. H. Addis in *The Argonaut.*

Thomas Allibone Janvier wrote a version of the La Llorona story for a 1906 issue of Harper's Magazine:

As is generally known, Señor, many bad things are met with by night in the streets of the City; but this Wailing Woman, La Llorona, is the very worst of them all. She is worse by far than the vaca de lumbre—that at midnight comes forth from the potrero of San Pablo and goes galloping through the streets like a blazing whirlwind, breathing forth from her nostrils smoke and sparks and flames: because the Fiery Cow, Señor, while a dangerous animal to look at, really does no harm whatever—and La Llorona is as harmful as she can be!

Seeing her walking quietly along the quiet street—at the times when she is not running, and shrieking for her lost children—she seems a respectable person, only odd looking because of her white petticoat and the white reboso with which her head is covered, and anybody might speak to her. But whoever does speak to her, in that very same moment dies!

The beginning of her was so long ago that no one knows when was the beginning of her; nor does any one know anything about her at all. But it is known certainly that at the beginning of her, when she was a living woman, she committed bad sins. As soon as ever a child was born to her she would throw it into one of the canals which surround the City, and so would drown it; and she had a great many children, and this practice in regard to them she continued for a long time. At last her conscience began to prick her about what she did with her children; but whether it was that the priest spoke to her, or that some of the saints cautioned her in the matter, no one knows. But it is certain that because of her sinnings she began to go through the streets in the darkness weeping and wailing. And presently it was said that from night till morning there was a wailing woman in the streets; and to see her, being in terror of her, many people went forth at midnight; but none did see her, because she could be seen only when the street was deserted and she was alone.

Sometimes she would come to a sleeping watchman, and would waken him by asking: "What time is it?" And he would see a woman clad in white standing beside him with her reboso drawn over her face. And he would answer: "It is twelve hours of the night." And she would say: "At twelve hours of this day I must be in Guadalajara!"—or it might be in San Luis Potosí, or in some other far-distant city—and, so speaking, she would shriek bitterly: "Where shall I find my children?"—and would vanish instantly and utterly away. And the watchman would feel as though all his senses had gone from him, and would become as a dead man. This happened many times to many watchmen, who made report of it to their officers; but their officers would not believe what they told. But it happened, on a night, that an officer of the watch was passing by the lonely street beside the church of Santa Anita. And there he met with a woman wearing a white reboso and a white petticoat; and to her he began to make love. He urged her, saying: "Throw off your reboso that I may see your pretty face!" And suddenly she uncovered her face—and what he beheld was a bare grinning skull set fast to the bare bones of a skeleton! And while he looked at her, being in horror, there came from her fleshless jaws an icy breath; and the iciness of it froze the very heart's blood in him, and he fell to the earth heavily in a deathly swoon. When his senses came back to him he was greatly troubled. In fear he returned to the Diputacion, and there told what had befallen him. And in a little while his life forsook him and he died.

What is most wonderful about this Wailing Woman, Señor, is that she is seen in the same moment by different people in places widely apart: one seeing her hurrying across the atrium of the Cathedral;

another beside the Arcos de San Cosme; and yet another near the Salto del Agua, over by the prison of Belen. More than that, in one single night she will be seen in Monterey and in Oaxaca and in Acapulco–the whole width and length of the land apart–and whoever speaks with her in those far cities, as here in Mexico, immediately dies in fright. Also, she is seen at times in the country. Once some travellers coming along a lonely road met with her, and asked: "Where go you on this lonely road?" And for answer she cried: "Where shall I find my children?" and, shrieking, disappeared. And one of the travellers went mad. Being come here to the City they told what they had seen; and were told that this same Wailing Woman had maddened or killed many people here also.

Because the Wailing Woman is so generally known, Señor, and so greatly feared, few people now stop her when they meet with her to speak with her–therefore few now die of her, and that is fortunate. But her loud keen wailings, and the sound of her running feet, are heard often; and especially in nights of storm. I myself, Señor, have heard the running of her feet and her wailings; but I never have seen her. God forbid that I ever shall!

BIBLIOGRAPHY

Books

Alexander, Hartley Burr. *Latin American Mythology*. Boston, 1920.

Aragón, Ray John de. *The Legend of La Llorona*. Sunstone Press, 2006.

Bitto, Robert. *Mexican Monsters: The Cryptids and Legendary Creatures of Mexico*. Mexico Unexplained, 2019.

Bierhorst, John. *The Hungry Woman: Myths and Legends of the Aztec*. William Morrow & Co, 1984.

Birchell, Donna Blake. *Haunted Hotels and Ghostly Getaways of New Mexico*. The History Press, 2018.

Bowles, David. *Mexican Bestiary: Bestiario Mexicano*. Overlooked Books, 2016.

------------------. *Ghosts of the Rio Grande Valley*. The History Press, 2016.

Bullock, Alice. *Living Legends Of The Santa Fe Country: A Collection Of Southwestern Stories*. Green Mountain Press, 1970.

----------------- *The Squaw Tree*. The Lightning Tree, 1978.

Charles, Beula. *Tales of the Tularosa*. By the author, 1959.

Dobie, J. Frank. *Tongues of the Monte: The Mexico I Like*. Hammond, Hammond & Co., Ltd., 1948.

--------------------- *Puro Mexicano*. The Texas Folklore Society, 2000.

García, Nasario. *Brujerías: Stories of Witchcraft and the Supernatural in the American Southwest and Beyond.* Texas Tech University Press, 2007.

\-\-\-\-\-\-\-\-\-\-\-\-\-\-\-\-\-\-\- *Tales of Witchcraft and the Supernatural in the Pecos Valley.* Western Edge Press, 1999.

Hudnall, Ken & Sharon. *Spirits of the Border IV: The History and Mystery of New Mexico.* Omega Press, 2005.

Janvier, Thomas A. *Legends of the City of Mexico.* Kindle Edition, 2017.

Jaramillo, Cleofas M. *Shadows of the Past.* Ancient City Press, 1972.

Kluckhohn, Clyde. *Navaho Witchcraft.* Beacon Press, 1963.

Kraul, Edward Garcia and Judith Beatty. *The Weeping Woman: Encounters with La Llorona.* The Word Process, 1988.

Kutz, Jack. *Mysteries & Miracles of New Mexico.* Rhombus Press, 1988.

\-\-\-\-\-\-\-\-\-\-\-\- *Mysteries & Miracles of Texas.* Rhombus Press, 1994.

Moran, Mark and Wesley Treat. *Weird Texas.* Union Square & Co., 2005.

Murray, Earl. *Ghosts of the Old West.* Dorset Press, 1988.

Raynor, Ted. *The Gold Lettered Egg & other New Mexico Tales.* By the author, 1962.

Robe, Stanley L. *Hispanic Legends from New Mexico (Folklore and Mythology Studies: 31).* University of California Press, 1980.

Sinclair, John L. *Cowboy Riding Country.* University of New Mexico Press, 1982.

Skinner, Charles M. *Myths and Legends of Our Own Land.* J.B. Lippincott Company, 1896.

Snorf, Annie Laurie and Hazel Vineyard (Ed.). *Yucca Land: A Collection of the Folklore of New Mexico.* American Guild Press, 1958.

Waters, Stephanie. *Colorado Legends & Lore: The Phantom Fiddler, Snow Snakes and Other Tales.* The History Press, 2014.

Williams, Docia Shultz. *When Darkness Falls: Tales of San Antonio Ghosts and Hauntings.* Taylor Trade Publishing, 1997.

Articles

Bitto, Robert. "The Vampire Witches of Central Mexico." Mexico Unexplained (July 18, 2016) https://mexicounexplained.com/vampire-witches-central-mexico/

----------------- "The Mysterious Doña Marina, the Most Important Woman in Mexican History." Mexico Unexplained (June 13, 2016) https://mexicounexplained.com/mysterious-dona-marina-important-woman-mexican-history/

Espinosa, Aurelio M. "New-Mexican Spanish Folk-Lore" *The Journal of American Folklore* Vol. 23, No. 90 (Oct. - Dec. 1910).

Fuller, Dr. Amy. "La Llorona and the Days of the Dead." Mexico Lore. https://www.mexicolore.co.uk/aztecs/home/la-llorona-and-the-days-of-the-dead-in-mexico-1

Kirtley, Bacil F. "'La Llorona' and Related Themes." *Western Folklore*, Vol. 19, No. 3 (July 1960).

Leddy, Betty. "La Llorona in Southern Arizona." *Western Folklore*, Vol. 7, No. 3 (July 1948).

Matthews, W. "The prayer of a Navaho Shaman." *American Anthropologist* (vol. 1, no. 2 1888).

Sanchez, Lynda. "New Mexico's Weeping Woman." *Vision Magazine* (October 1, 1999).

Speer, Garilee. "Local ghost stories, sites delight Demingites." *The Deming Headlight* (October 31, 1994).

Winick, Stephen. "La Llorona: Roots, Branches, and the Missing Link from Spain." Library of Congress Blogs. https://blogs.loc.gov/folklife/2021/10/la-llorona-roots-branches-and-the-missing-link-from-spain/

Zumel, Nina. "The Tlahuelpuchi Epidemic." Multo Ghost. (September 10, 2015) https://multoghost.wordpress.com/2015/09/10/the-tlahuelpuchi-epidemic

INDEX

ABOUT THE AUTHOR

John LeMay was born and raised in Roswell, NM, the "UFO Capital of the World." He is the author of over 50 books, many of them on the history of the Southwest such as *Tall Tales and Half Truths of Billy the Kid*, and *Roswell USA: Towns That Celebrate UFOs, Lake Monsters, Bigfoot and Other Weirdness*. In addition to non-fiction, he is also the author of the novels *The Noted Desperado Pancho Dumez* and *Once Upon a Time in Fort Sumner*. He has also written for Western journals and magazines such as *True West*, *The Coalition Journal*, the *Tombstone Epitaph*, and the *Wild West History Association Journal*. He is a Past President of the Board of Directors for the Historical Society for Southeast New Mexico.

The following titles are available for purchase on Amazon.com, and are available to bookstores at a wholesale discount via Ingram Content Group (ISBNs of available editions listed for this purpose)

CRYPTOZOOLOGY/COWBOYS & SAURIANS

Cowboys & Saurians: Prehistoric Beasts as Seen by the Pioneers explores dinosaur sightings from the pioneer period via real newspaper reports from the time. Well-known cases like the Tombstone Thunderbird are covered along with more obscure cases like the Crosswicks Monster and more. Softcover (357 pp/5.06" X 7.8") Suggested Retail: $19.95 ISBN: 978-1-7341546-1-0

Cowboys & Saurians: Ice Age zeroes in on snowbound saurians like the Ceratosaurus of the Arctic Circle and a Tyrannosaurus of the Tundra, as well as sightings of Ice Age megafauna like mammoths, glyptodonts, Sarkastodons and Saber-toothed tigers. Tales of a land that time forgot in the Arctic are also covered. Softcover (264 pp/5.06" X 7.8") Suggested Retail: $14.99 ISBN: 978-1-7341546-7-2

Southerners & Saurians takes the series formula of exploring newspaper accounts of monsters in the pioneer period with an eye to the Old South. In addition to dinosaurs are covered Lizardmen, Frogmen, giant leeches and mosquitoes, and the Dingocroc, which might be an alien rather than a prehistoric survivor. Softcover (202 pp/5.06" X 7.8") Suggested Retail: $13.99 ISBN: 978-1-7344730-4-9

Cowboys & Saurians South of the Border explores the saurians of Central and South America, like the Patagonian Plesiosaurus that was really an Iemisch, plus tales of the Neo-Mylodon, a menacing monster from underground called the Minhocao, Glyptodonts, and even Bolivia's three-headed dinosaur! Softcover (412 pp/5.06"X7.8") Suggested Retail: $17.95 ISBN: 978-1-953221-73-5

UFOLOGY/THE REAL COWBOYS & ALIENS IN CONJUNCTION WITH ROSWELL BOOKS

The Real Cowboys and Aliens: Early American UFOs explores UFO sightings in the USA between the years 1800-1864. Stories of encounters sometimes involved famous figures in U.S. history such as Lewis and Clark, and Thomas Jefferson.Hardcover (242pp/6" X 9") Softcover (262 pp/5.06" X 7.8") Suggested Retail: $24.99 (hc)/$15.95(sc) ISBN: 978-1-7341546-8-9\(hc)/978-1-7344730-8-7(sc)

The second entry in the series, Old West UFOs, covers reports spanning the years 1865-1895. Includes tales of Men in Black, Reptilians, Spring-Heeled Jack, Sasquatch from space, and other alien beings, in addition to the UFOs and airships. Hardcover (276 pp/6" X 9") Softcover (308 pp/5.06" X 7.8") Suggested Retail: $29.95 (hc)/$17.95(sc) ISBN: 978-1-7344730-0-1 (hc)/ 978-1-7344730-2-5 (sc)

The third entry in the series, The Coming of the Airships, encompasses a short time frame with an incredibly high concentration of airship sightings between 1896-1899. The famous Aurora, Texas, UFO crash of 1897 is covered in depth along with many others. Hardcover (196 pp/6" X 9") Softcover (222 pp/5.06" X 7.8") Suggested Retail: $24.99 (hc)/$15.95(sc) ISBN: 978-1-7347816 -1-8 (hc)/978-1-7347816-0-1(sc)

Featuring cases the authors missed, The Lost Cases covers things such as the skyquakes recorded by Lewis and Clark, airships and the Spanish American War, Pancho Villa and crystal skulls, lost alien tribe of the Tundra, invisible alien monsters, the Great Moon Hoax of 1835, hellhounds and airships, the Sonora Airship Club and more. Softcover (252 pp/5.06" X 7.8") Suggested Retail: $18.99 ISBN: 978-1-953221-55-1

Cowboys & Saurians: Dinosaurs Down Under takes the series to Australia to explore tales of the cattle devouring Burrunjor, the dreaded Diprotodon, the terrible Tantanoola Tiger, the marsupial Sasquatch known as the Yowie, plus Thylacines, Bunyips, giant rabbits, Megalodons and dinosaurs in nearby New Zealand. Softcover (240 pp/ 5.06" X 7.8") Suggested Retail: $14.95 ISBN: 978-1-953221-34-6

As the title suggest, Cowboys & Saurians in the Modern Era takes the series into the 20th Century with tales of the Texas Pterosaur flap of 1976, the Bladenboro Beast of the 1950s, the Busco Turtle Beast of the 1940s, dinosaur sightings in the Great Depression and far out tales of mini-mastodons, dinosaur men, and Snallygasters. Softcover (320 pp/ 5.06" X 7.8") Suggested Retail: $19.95 ISBN: 978-1-953221-22-3

Settlers & Serpents wrangles the best "Snaik Stories" of the Southwest and beyond in a single volume. Whether it's simple giant snakes or lake serpents, they're corralled in the pages within. Also included are entries on the Leviathan in Mesoamerica and the Southwest plus a detailed look at the giant rattlesnake of Pecos Pueblo. Softcover (180 pp/ 5.06" X 7.8") Suggested Retail: $14.99 ISBN: 978-1-953221-21-6

Written for young readers ages 9-12, Monsters of the Old South collects the best creature stories of the swamplands including White River Monster, Green Eyes, the Crocodingo, the Averasboro Gallinipper, the Tennessee Snake Woman, the Arkansas Gowrow, Bigfoot in the Mississippi River and more. Softcover (122 pp/4.25" X 7") Suggested Retail: $12.99 ISBN: 978-17347816-9-4

Early 20th Century UFOs kicks off a new series that investigates UFO sightings of the early 1900s. Includes tales of UFOs sighted over the Titanic as it sunk, Nikola Tesla receiving messages from the stars, an alien being found encased in ice, and a possible virus from outer space!Hardcover (196 pp/6" X 9") Softcover (222 pp/5.06" X 7.8") Suggested Retail: $27.99 (hc)/$16.95(sc) ISBN: 978-1-7347816-1-8 (hc)/978-1-73478 16-0-1(sc)

UFOs in the Roaring Twenties takes a look at UFO sightings in the 1920s just as the title suggests, along with accounts of Mothman in Nebraska, Lincoln LaPaz's first UFO case, Men in Black investigating an airship crash in Braxton County, West Virginia, Camden's Cosmic Sniper, and much more! Softcover (248 pp/5.06" X 7.8") Suggested Retail: $19.99 ISBN: 978-1-953221-51-3

UFOs of the Turbulent Thirties concludes the authors' investigation of the last unexplored decade of Ufology in the Great Depression with accounts of Mothman, Ghost Fliers, Nazi Bells, the Underground City of the Lizard People, a vanished village on the tundra, and even gangsters and aliens. Softcover (212 pp/5.06" X 7.8") Suggested Retail: $17.95 ISBN: 978-1-953221-35-3

Written for young readers ages 9-12, Space Monsters of the Old West collects the best alien sightings of the Wild West including Mummies from Mars, Bigfoot from the Moon, Pascagoula's space ghouls, the Crawfordsville Monster, Spring-Heeled Jack, the dinosaurian alien creatures that invaded Van Meter, Iowa. Softcover (120 pp/4.25" X 7") Suggested Retail: $12.99 ISBN: 978-1-953221-87-2

COWBOYS & MONSTERS

Cowboys & Monsters features potentially true stories of real vampires, werewolves, and even mummies unique to America's Wild West period. Examples include the cursed mummy of John Wilkes Booth, New Orleans immortal vampire Jacques St. Germain, precursors to the Beast of Bray Road, and the origins of Skinwalker Ranch. Softcover (316 pp/5.06" X 7.8") Suggested Retail: $19.99 ISBN: 978-1-953221-46-9

The first entry in this trilogy of non-fiction terror sinks its teeth into the lore of the vampire in North America and Mexico, with detailed rundowns on the vampire hunters of Exeter, Rhode Island, a tribe of Bat People, the nocturnal shape-shifting vampire witches of Tlaxcala, the immortal ways of Comte St. Germain in New Orleans and more. Softcover (200 pp/ 5.06" X 7.8") Suggested Retail: $12.99 ISBN: 978-1-953221-38-4

Mummies of the Americas explores Death Valley's city of the Dead, King Tut's Tomb along the Arkansas, the Egyptian City of the Grand Canyon plus the famous mummies of John Wilkes Boothe, Elmer McCurdy, the Cardiff Giant, the Mummy of Helldorado, and even Billy the Kid's pickled trigger finger! Softcover (200 pp/5.06" X 7.8") Suggested Retail: $12.99 ISBN: 978-1-953221-37-7

Cowboys & Dogmen is devoted to tales of werewolves of the Wild West including the dreaded Navajo skinwalker, the Watrous Werewolf, the Beast of the Land Between the Lakes, the Hellhounds of El Dorado Canyon, the dreaded Dog Eater, the Wahhoo, the Wolf Man of Versailles, the Michigan Dog-Man and more! Softcover (212 pp/5.06" X 7.8") Suggested Retail: $12.99 ISBN: 978-1-953221-36-0

FICTION/ MISC. HISTORY

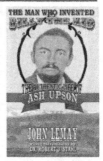

The first novel from historian John LeMay weaves a fantastic web of fiction via real life mysteries and legends of New Mexico, namely the puzzling theft and return of Billy the Kid's tombstone in 1976, the legend of the Lost Adams Diggings, the villainous Santa Fe Ring, and the enigmatic Acoma Mesa. Softcover (250 pp/5.5" X 7.5") Suggested Retail: $14.95 ISBN: 978-1-953221-42-1

The year is 1950, and old timers connected to the long-dead outlaw Billy the Kid are turning up murdered in New Mexico. Some blame the killings on the avenging witch of the Navajo nation, the skinwalker, while others think it's no coincidence that a man claiming to be a surviving Billy the Kid is set to meet with the governor soon... Softcover (260 pp/5.5" X 7.5") Suggested Retail: $16.95 ISBN: 978-1-953221-32-2

Roswell, USA, the long-forgotten debut work of John LeMay, is available again and covers the minutia of the infamous Roswell UFO Crash of 1947. Notable chapters include tales of an alien ghost haunting the old airbase, monsters in the nearby Bottomless Lakes, and even a dinosaur sighting outside of town. Softcover (248 pp/6" X 9") Suggested Retail: $14.95 ISBN: 978-0-9817597-5-3

This biography, for the first time ever, tells the history of western journalist Ash Upson, who ghostwrote Pat Garrett's *The Authentic Life of Billy the Kid* in 1882 and also reproduces many of Upson's letters that detailed the harsh realities of frontier life in New Mexico during the turbulent Lincoln County War. Softcover (318 pp/5.5" X 8.5") Suggested Retail: $16.99 ISBN: 978-1953221919

THE NEW MEXICO BOOK OF

WITCHES

JOHN LEMAY

Made in the USA
Monee, IL
04 September 2024

64369907R00105